Charles Edward Pickett

Philosopher Pickett's anti-plundercrat Pamphlet

Charles Edward Pickett

Philosopher Pickett's anti-plundercrat Pamphlet

ISBN/EAN: 9783337070601

Printed in Europe, USA, Canada, Australia, Japan

Cover: Foto ©ninafisch / pixelio.de

More available books at **www.hansebooks.com**

Philosopher Pickett's

Anti-Plundercrat

Pamphlet.

That country only is well governed whose Philosophers are its rulers
or whose rulers philosophise.—*Plato.*

San Francisco, June, 1873.

INTRODUCTION.

The Constitutional election is over. That popular verdict has been rendered aright. The question arises—what has been gained thereby? A new State chart has been substituted for the old; one piece of paper in the place of another. Is this to be all? If the old one failed to guard the rights of the masses, in consequence of its wilful and unwilful perversion by those entrusted with its interpretation and enforcement, will not the new be equally ignored or perverted should the same description of men be chosen to occupy our public stations? It will. Hence, the election in September is of more practical importance than that transpiring the 7th of May. At the latter the people selected but a piece of *machinery*. In September they have to select competent *machinists* and *engineers* to put that machinery in working order, and run it on the track of truth. If they fail to make such proper selections, then will they become co-responsible with the opposing party, should anarchy and a sanguinary conclusion result. This latter alternative is imminent. To it we are rapidly drifting. Antidotes to avert such direful danger must speedily be administered. As yet the selfishly blinded plunderocracy talk only of physical force repression, in the event their lavish outlaying of money, to corrupt the ballot, shall fail them. Their defeat the 7th of May will but inspire them to still greater exertions to prevent the election of good men in September. New and desperate devices will be resorted to to achieve a victory then and create a reactionary tide in their favor. Should their candidates be defeated they will next, as heretofore, bring the power of their ill-gotten gold to corrupt the representatives chosen. Should they fail in this, then will they, co-operating with the plundercrats East, use every exertion to elect a President subservient to their purposes, who, of necessity, will, like the Czar of Russia, declare martial law and raise great armies and a vast police force to put down opposition to the *bourgeoisie* oligarchy. The recent veto by President Hayes, at the ordering of the plunderocracy and Republican malignants

East, of the bill repealing the army election police, is a portion of the programme paving the way for the contemplated military government.

The night I delivered my discourse in Metropolitan Temple, a big burly "capitalist," as I took him to be, remained, after the others had departed, to say, in a menacing tone and manner to me, that such sentiments as I had uttered would not much longer be tolerated ; that if not otherwise suppressed, martial law would be proclaimed.

In truth, the outlook for the successful application of peaceful remedies is not encouraging. The wealthy *bourgeoisie* will refuse to abate their predacious practices or permit, if possible, the curtailment of their oppressive power.

The rapidly increasing impoverished and defrauded many grow daily more embittered, and will listen little to arguments favoring a joint control of the Government, but seek absolute supremacy for themselves ; the more encouraged and incited to this by reason of having their resentments inflamed by the sneers and taunts and insulting epithets applied to them by these moneycrats and their minions. Instead of holding out the olive branch of peace, and agreeing, in good faith, to abide the decision of the Grand Comitia on the 7th of May, they have determined to still pursue their " bulldosing " programme of discharging employees, getting up a business panic, depressing all values, and increasing the money scarcity, in hopes of yet compelling the masses to succumb to them, and keep in ascendancy their robber rule.

At the same time, amid these contending factions, portentous antagonisms and bad-blooded disputations of classes, our leading politicians, all over the Republic, are too unknowing or too timid (selfishly fearing the loss of popularity) to come forward and assist in proposing and establishing a sound reconstructed governmental plan, and measures of reconciliation and permanent adjustment.

These bat-blinded Bourbons and selfish office-seekers, apparently ignorant of the fact that we are entering a new and startling revolutionary era, in America, pregnant with mighty events, which find no parallel in our history, are consoling themselves with the belief, and so expressing it, that this new upheaval is but spasmodic and destined to be of ephemeral duration. Poor drivilling fools! None of them appear to apprehend the vast significance of the momentous contest we have already entered upon in California, which contest is destined to early extend over the entire continent, the first pitched battle in which, after a few preliminary skirmishes, being fought the 7th of May; a day destined to be memorable in American annals long ages hence; a day which will enthuse millions of the enwronged, and terrorise their wrongers throughout all Christendom, so soon as men find out the great, the living, the fundamental issues at stake on that epochal Wednesday.

In my discourse I cite from sacred and profane history parallel examples to prove on which side the ultimate victory will lie—on which the God of Hosts as well as the heaviest battalions will be found.

The arrogant and offensive expressions of the plundercrats and their organs since their recent repulse, indicate that other and fiercer struggles must be had before their Waterloo defeat shall have been reached. Immediately succeeding the election, they defiantly threw down the gage of battle to re-contest the issue in September. We are prepared to meet them. It is to be presumed that no one who voted for the New Constitution will so stultify himself as to vote for a candidate who opposed it.

As stated in my discourse, the old parties are utterly broken to pieces in this State, and that voters were then taking such sides as would determine their future action. Of course, some thousands of the riff-raff negatives and cowardly selfish, will gravitate now to the victorious party. Whatever shams and subterfuges may be put forth by the Democratic and Republican party leaders (all being in the service and pay of the plundercrats) their forces will be, *sub rosa*, united at the ides of September to steal a victory and undo, as far as possible, the popular decreement of the 7th of May, should they then succeed. Every candidate nominated and arranged to receive their joint vote, by such secret coalition, whether entitled Democrat, Republican, Non-Partisan or otherwise, will, of necessity, be a sworn servitor of the plunderocracy.

This new enranking of the various plundercratic cohorts, will, necessitate a closer reunion and consolidation of the opposing forces. (See Appendix B.)

Merchant Coleman's sneering allusion to the "Unthinking Majority" was the truth ; otherwise, would such majority not, these many years, have suffered themselves to be suicidally hoodwinked and used by Coleman and his kind.

But such majority are beginning to think. Their vote the 7th of May attests this. Let them give further evidence of such awakened mentality by perusing, attentively, the matter in these pages, and acting in accordance with its suggestion. It is voiced by one who, all during the thirty years supremacy of the plunderocracy in California, has, unceasingly, combatted their wicked system and still more wicked instruments.

My discourse was prepared less for effect in the recent campaign than the existing and future ones. In truth, it is an exegesis or unfolding of legal axioms and economic principles, interspersed with allegations of important facts and expositions of personal characters and antecedents to illustrate my general theme and better inform my fellow-citizens as to their rights and duty.

The vote at the late election demonstrates the existence of three great classes or social components in California.

1st. The *Bourgeoisie*, which includes the bankers, merchants, stock operators, land speculators, franchised incorporators, and other "business" or monied element, together with their adherents. These all opposed the New Constitution— and for three principal reasons—that if adopted, together with the accordant legislation of its supporters, it would stop their stealing, compel the disgorgement of much of their plunder in hand, and send hundreds of their leading men into self-banishment or quarters in the State Prison.

2d. The *Proletariat* or common laboring element of the

cities, including the various mechanical guilds, etc. These were nearly all at heart, in favor of the New Constitution, but many coerced, by employers, to vote against it, else refrain from voting.

3d. The Agricultural, which, mostly, sanctioned the New Constitution.

The interests of the two latter are largely identified, and being equally oppressed and depredated upon by the first, they "pooled their issues" and won a victory. The difficulty, in the future, will be to keep these in harmonious relations. Should either attempt to dictate the policy or selection of candidates of a joint ruling party, there will be divergence between them. To encourage this jealousy and antagonism, is now the endeavor of the *bourgeoisie*.

"Divide and conquer," is their determined policy. In this they will succeed should not a lofty spirit of self-abnegation, and wise and patriotic appreciation animate and enlighten the leading man entrusted with the all important responsibility of selecting candidates for office.

In my discourse I have portrayed the order of men to select, and how to know them. If such candidates be not sought and selected on their merit alone, then will the New Constitution advocates speedily disintegrate instead of crystallising into a powerful, permanent and dominant party. Then will be consummated the ardently hoped for result indicated in a leading *bourgeoisie* journal of this city (the *Bulletin*), which reads : "It is exceedingly problematical whether it (the New Party) can stand the disintegrating effects of an eager scramble for the offices. As soon as it comes to a division of the expected spoils, centrifugal forces will come into play."

But I cannot believe that this great uprising of the people of California will tolerate such a result.

The *Bulletin* and all of *its* party are influenced alone by such sordid, selfish and dishonest motives. Their unparalleled lying and other foul appliances resorted to, in the late campaign to obtain a victory; and the same tactics determined on, for the future, stamp them with such characteristics.

If however, the party of reform are still too blind to perceive whom to choose for office, then let there be still further upheavings and convulsions; let anarchy, for a season, have sway and blood oblations drench the land, since in such purifying and enlightening eras as try the souls of the affrighted and mad-passioned multitude will the master minds be known.

In the discourse, I have cautioned our party against that class of tide-waiting demagogues, who watch the ebbing and flowing of the popular current to jump in, at the propitious turn, in order to be wafted into some official position, to feed on pap and plunder in pastures new. Some specimen names of this class, who have recently pushed themselves forward, are given, and more such will be exposed if put forward for official stations, or officiously intruding themselves in the front. *Every candidate must have a cleanly record.*

It is equally important to guard against the treachery and untrustworthiness of those newspapers, which, after battling for years, as obedient mouth-pieces of the plunderocracy, *apparently* abandon the service of their old masters, at the eleventh hour, to become loud-mouthed "reformers." A notorious strumpet may honestly reform her ways, and preach chastity to her sex; but society will not permit her to be enranked on equality, much less become a leader among the always virtuous, and be entrusted with the instruction, care and guidance of unsophisticated girls. Additional to the taint attaching to her, she may backslide, and carry some of those girls with her; and so it is with these newly reformed political and journalistic bawds. Beware of them !

This pamphlet is necessarily placed on sale, the expenses attending the delivery of the discourse and its publication having run me in debt some hundreds of dollars.

I have given away nearly all my writings; have expended thousands of dollars in printing newspapers, pamphlets, and circulars, additional to the vast amount of gratis contributions to many journals. After losing through lavish expending, and inattention to private affairs, to devote myself to public ones, a once ample fortune, honorably acquired, and being swindled out of another by the plundercrats, through the instrumentality of their venal agents, the judiciary, the same spirit which prompted Marat to pawn the sheets from his bed, to pay for continuing the publication of his paper, impelled me, on more than one occasion, to pawn a portion of my scanty wardrobe to raise the money to print my free distributed pamphlets, advocating the same ideas, principles and purposes enunciated in this.

Now, that the people of California, after their lengthy servile acquiesence, are revolting against the misrule of the plundercrats, and better hearkening to the promulgators of such sentiments, I intend, if sufficiently assisted, to republish some of those writings, as a guide to their future actions. Some extracts from two of my pamphlets are inserted in this.

In conclusion, permit me to express my joy at the auspicious dawning of a better day, albeit years, yet, of expiatory suffering and purifying troublous times must ensue, as bounden effects of the long period of scourging misrule, which has afflicted the land. All during this period have I battled against such wrong-doing, greatly jeopardizing my life thereby, (preserved by my ever attending and guarding good spirit), accepted, for years, poverty, bodily deprivations and private station, in place of fortune, ease and high preferment, which could have been mine, had I chosen to abjure my faith, compromise my honor, and give adhesion to the reigning regime.

For long long years did I endure much agony of spirit at witnessing so much of wrong and untruth, and the apathy of my fellow citizens in permitting, nay, worse, nearly all participating in it. But through these encompassing dangers and sore heart tribulations I have safely passed the fiery ordeal of temptations few mortals have been subjected to. Though ofttimes made grievously soul sick at the deferred hope of a reawakening of my countrymen to more patriotic and virtuous thoughts and deeds, I have never despaired of this awakening, because a full believer in the rising and the reigning again of imperishable TRUTH, however much and long crushed down. I have ever had faith in GOD—in the justice of HEAVEN—in the ultimate triumph of RIGHT.

The pamphlet has been rendered more voluminous than it otherwise would, for the reason that there is not a paper in San Francisco, nor, perhaps, in all California, in the columns of which can be published an able and impartial article on public affairs, especially, if emanating from my pen; hence, such matter must appear through pamphlet medium or not at all.

I have, likewise, made more, seemingly, egotistical allusions to myself, for the same reason, than I would otherwise have done. I have only uttered the truth thereabout, and but a small portion of such truth at that; whilst these cowardly, corrupt and defamatory newspapers have only had language of detraction, or gibberish ridicule to employ towards me. I pray that none of them will, in future, cast any reflection upon my character by praising me. Their years of slanderous outgivings regarding me has never troubled me except to grieve that such has so greatly forestalled my influence by preventing my countrymen more heeding the many wisdom lessons I have always taught them. Instead of permitting the logic of their intellects to judge the merits of my productions, they accepted the *ipse dixit* of these mercenary sheets, that such being the emanations of an impracticable eccentric or semi-insane person no regard should be paid to them.

I await to see how many of these journals will speak aright respecting the contents of these pages; and I hope that everybody having the good of society at heart, who may peruse them, will, also, observe the same.

A DISCOURSE

ON

LAW, JUDGES, LAWYERS, Et al.

THE PEOPLE versus THE PLUNDERCRATS.

Impending Downfall of the Bourgeoisie Power.

KEARNEYISM ANALYSED.

[Delivered in Metropolitan Temple, San Francisco, April 28th, 1879.]

I have captioned my discourse, in legal style, as suitable to the subject-matter. The *et al.* affords me a wide range to discuss men and things. I avail myself of the privilege.

Plunderocracy is a term of my own coinage, and frequently used in my writings of late years. It is compounded of an English and a Greek word, signifying the rule of plunderers. California, from its organization, has been absolutely under their control. This hellish and impoverishing power is about to be overthrown.

In opening my discourse, I present a brief outline of the general indictment against them. I arraign, as a self-constituted Prosecuting Attorney, these great criminals at the bar of PUBLIC OPINION.

The Plundercrats have poisoned the fountains of Justice—have prostituted, to subserve their nefarious purposes, our high and low officials, and spread doubt, disaffection and distress throughout the entire State. They have destroyed public confidence, and brought blight and mildew upon a land blessed with an unequaled climate and unsurpassed natural resources. They have aggregated, and are aggregating, through the medium of perverted law and corrupt public officials, the wealth produced by the many, into the possession of the non-producing few. They have undermined the foundations of the social system, and endangered the existence of our governmental structure. They have trampled truth beneath their feet, denounced every virtuous person in the community, ignored God and set up the "golden calf" for their sole worship as well as ours. Judging all others by themselves, they have declared there is no virtue in any—that every one has his price, and thus inculcated a deep and all-pervading, demoralized sentiment throughout society, which has induced thousands, who would otherwise have remained uncontaminated, to barter principle for place and pelf, or forfeit their honor, otherwise. Rather than abate any of their evil practices, or surrender any portion of their usurped power and accumulated plunder, they have resolved, in concertment with their bandit brethren East, to plunge the country into anarchy to maintain such usurpation through the establishment of a military despotism. To this end they are centering upon General Grant as the most available candidate and reliable chieftain for President ; designing that he shall, if elected, re-enact the *role* of Cæsar Augustus, in artfully veiling his actions beneath the forms of the Republic, yet exercising imperatorial power.

To still further parallel the Roman prototypes, we have Grant, already, re-enacting the role of Julius Cæsar in "thrice refusing the Crown"—that is, declining to become a Presidential Candidate.

Law, in the phraseology of Blackstone, is defined to be— "A rule of civil conduct prescribed by the supreme power in a State, commanding what is right and prohibiting what is wrong." This signifies constitutional and statutory enactments, which are never made perfect in any land, and fall far short of being so in America, of late years.

Our laws, however, are greatly better than their administra-

tion; especially here in California, where a derelict judiciary
have perverted their meaning, in order to construe them in
favor of that *spider* portion of society, who weave their legal
webs to entangle victims and suck away their substance. In
truth, this gross perversion of law in our State, from its foundation (against which I have always fiercely battled,) has
rendered justice a mockery, and made the name of judge and
lawyer a synonym for knave.

Law is the loftiest of all the sciences, since it is the
guardian of man's rights, the conservator of his morals, and
prescriber of his civil duties. Yet, how few professional
lawyers in our land, these latter days, appear to realize such
high significance, else would they better study and more rely
upon the great elementary principles and ethical inculcations
of this science—upon which all justice is founded—instead of
resorting to petty quibblings about defects in each other's
pleadings, to squabblings as to the meaning of words and
phrases in the statutes, and trickery and claptrap to circum-
vent each other in court proceedings. But such practice will
prevail as long as this class of lawyers, or, more properly
speaking, attorneys, shall be elevated to judicial stations, who
license and encourage such pettifogging perversion of genuine
law. Such never rise above mouthings about the Practice Act
or verbal tweedledums and tweedledees, and are incapable of
comprehending arguments deduced from the spirit of laws,
which is the essence of justice.

Law, in its elementary signification, is the perfection of
reason, or unadulterated common-sense. It is synonymous
with TRUTH, RIGHT, JUSTICE.

It may, also, be defined as LOGIC. Hence, the logical mind
will, always, arrive at just conclusions and expound the law as
it should be. And he has the best judicial intellect who, gifted
with good perception and love of truth, shall strive to
render justice between man and man. This, one may be, and
has often proved to be, who never perused a law book page.

All just statutory law is evolved from and based upon
natural law. Therefore, whatever is right is law ; law in the
abstract, which should be made consonant in the concrete—
that is, law in its true and righteous signification. But law as

dispensed in California, has, in the main, been divorced from justice.

The philosophical and analytical intellect is enabled, through intuitive perception and by direct logical deductions, to arrive at correct conclusions, even if deficient in knowledge of the letter of the laws and Court rules and routine. The book teachings and forensic practice of the professional lawyer—undigested and indiscriminated—lead many of our judges further away from just judgments than if they had not read a line of such law.

The fact is, the larger portion of our practicing attorneys are wholly unfitted, by nature, to become lawyers. The bent of their genius lies in other directions. Whilst, unfortunately, the most of our so called leading lawyers, those who have acknowledged ability in their profession, have long been the unscrupulous employees of our plundercratic masters, exerting all their ingenuity, native talent, wicked wit and knowledge of the letter of the law, to secure unjust decisions in favor of such employers. These prominent members of the San Francisco Bar have been a terrible curse to the country. Courting their less talented brothers on the Bench, in order to gain favor in open Court, and secure private conferences with them, the better to bamboozle, or, failing this, to bribe them into giving judgment in favor of their thieving clients, the larger portion of the wrongdoing this State has groaned beneath, can justly be laid at their doors. Several such have acquired the infamous *soubriquet* of " Supreme Court Brokers."

I have long believed that a portion of our Supreme Court Justices should be laymen or non-professional lawyers.

The people of California, possibly, would have selected two or three, of the soon to be elected seven new Justices of this tribunal, from the laymen ranks, but for the legal gentlemen in the Constitutional Convention inserting a clause declaring all ineligible to such position unless professional attorneys admitted to practice in the Supreme Court. This rigid rule will even exclude, from candidacy, some talented attorneys.

I do not argue against a thorough book acquaintance of the law. The conscientious and naturally legal mind is all the wiser from such acquisition; but this book knowledge has been so prostituted in California, that I often think that if there had been no law books here, none, at least, accessible to the majority of our judges, especially those of the Supreme Court, we would have been blessed with more justice. For it appears that the most of their labored researches, in rummaging among the musty tomes of the law libraries, to hunt up " precedents " and " authorities " and "analogies," have been to discover pleas for deciding unjustly instead of justly, to bolster their predetermined inequitable decisions; and these, unhappily, I repeat, are the ones oftenest rendered by the major portion of them; in fact by a majority of judges throughout the land, since we came under the absolute dominion of the plunderocracy, whose creatures these judges are, and who adduce all the nice points of the law, all the doubtful, false or unapplicable precedents and authorities, and quote the same, along with a wordy outflow of jesuitical, double-dealing and dust-hiding jargon of their own, in order to mystify and misconstrue the statutes or papers of the parties litigant, to favor the speculator and monopolist. When it is a rich man or corporation, *versus* a poor man, the latter, almost, invariably, goes to the wall in these latter day American Courts.

For forty years and over, have nearly all laws in the United States, been made and administered—through lawyer instrumentality—to discriminate in favor of the trafficing, speculating and monopolizing non-producer, and against the producer.

The recently drafted Constitution, soon to be voted on by the people, will, undoubtedly, be adopted by a large majority. It is a good instrument, as compared with the generality of American State Constitutions—in fact, a great improvement upon them all. Of course there are defects in it, but I would have voted for it had it been far more defective than it is, if, for no other reason than to sweep from office, the justices of the Supreme Court, its legal and illegal ones, its drunken and its sober ones;

and the hold-over senators—base and perjured servitors of the plunderocracy.

The New Constitution is pronounced by the plundercratic organs and other supporters of theirs, to be radically defective in every particular, a communistic and revolutionary instrument. But how comes it, that with only fifty of the one-hundred and fifty-two delegates to the convention belonging to the Workingmen Party, (who, alone, are termed communists, and also characterised as asses), were enabled to dictate to, and out-vote the one hundred and two " conservative and talented " delegates, sent there by the other parties ? And how comes it that numbers of these latter, who were well pleased with their labors, and appended their signatures to the instrument, are now found opposing its adoption ?

Of what efficacy, however, are the best of Constitutions unless the right sort of men shall be selected to make, construe, and execute the laws ? The existing Constitution was good enough, perhaps, at least, for the first twenty years of the period it has served us; yet, of what little benefit has it been, as a palladium in defending the right and preventing the wrong; for the reason, that the larger portion of our law-makers and dispensers, from its adoption, have proved faithless to its provisions. This has been, especially true of that potent and polluted tribunal, the Supreme Court. It is highly proper to have Governors and Legislators, good men and true; but as these judges, of last resort, can undo or render null the good work of the law-making department, the welfare of all are at their mercy. Of what avail, I reiterate, the best of Constitutions and statute laws if an enlightened, conscientious, and firm judiciary, shall not be chosen to interpret them ? Great Britain has no written Constitution, yet mark the impartial administration of law in that realm. This arises from the fact that they there select for judicial stations, men of high moral worth and sound judgment, many of them not professional lawyers. A good thing in the New Constitution—additional to certain checks placed upon the judges in it, is in the supervising and restraining power lodged in the Legislature over the Supreme Court.

A great evil in our land lies in electing too many professional

lawyers to the Federal and State Legislatures, and in placing
none but practising attorneys on the higher Court benches,
entangled as are the most of these in California, in that debas-
ing American practice of champerty, which should render
such as are guilty of it, ineligible to these latter stations.
Champerty in England is declared, by law, a penal offense
and disbars a barrister. It should be so in our country, and it
is a great defect in the new, as well as old Constitution, that it
is not declared a felony, but it may be so declared by legislation. The law ought, likewise, to better regulate attorney's
fees. Clients are too much at the mercy of extortionate
counsel. Should an exhorbitant fee be demanded and refused,
what chance has a client in a suit brought for its recovery;
since it is a rule among the fraternity to swear, as experts, in
favor of the attorney's bill. In truth, nearly all will, as readily
and unscrupulously thus uphold a brother limb of the law as a
San Francisco policeman will perjure himself to screen or
extricate from some rascality, one of his number. But more,
at another time, about these latter lying myrmidons of the
plunderocracy.

The chief power—legitimate and usurped—of our State
government, lies in the Supreme Court; and its influence,
direct and indirect, is wielded for good or evil over every other
department and down to the lowest public official. The wide-
spread corruption and malfeasance in such other departments,
especially in the grossly criminal conduct of so many San
Francisco officials, is largely attributable to the example set
by the majority of Justices who have disgraced this high seat
in California. That deep depravity—that all-pervading laxity
of morals and prevalence of crime among the masses in our
State, is, likewise, largely owing to this dishonored tribunal—
since
>   " Thieves for their robbery have authority,
>   When judges steal, themselves."   SHAKESPEARE.

Instead of being a terror to evil-doers, these men of high
authority have encouraged them to proceed with impunity, in
their career of crime. True, they will often punish little

rogues with much severity, but always throw the protecting folds of their soiled ermine around the big ones.

A majority of the first Bench of Supreme Justices in this State (Bennett and Lyon), were proof against the bribes and other appliances brought to bear to induce them to decide unjustly ; but when these left that Bench in 1852, the next was *packed* with three obedient servitors of the Plunderocracy; and from that day to the present, such stenchy tribunal has always had a majority, and several times (as now) a full Bench corruptly acquiescent to the behests of the Plunderocracy.

The first Chief Justice was S. C. Hastings, founder of the Hastings Law College—as corrupt a judge as ever sat upon a Bench. He then and there laid the foundation of his colossal fortune, by selling his decisions right and left. Finding out how his honorable Associates were going to decide, he made merchandise of such knowledge by contracting with the winning suitors, to receive so much money for a favorable decision. And this notorious Plundercrat has been one of the " Brokers" for that Bench ever since.

Not alone are property rights insecure, being constantly invaded by badly framed and worsely construed and executed laws in California, but personal rights, the liberty of the individual and his political and other privileges have, in numerous instances, been grossly violated by judicial and executive officers. Neither established usages, the common law nor express statutory provisions have been any shield against such abuses, practiced by unfaithful officials, under the forms of law or asserted official authority, who have obeyed the behests of the plundercrats instead of the true mandates of the law and just monitions of their conscience.

Had the people of California elevated me to a seat on the Supreme Court Bench some years ago, although not educated in the legal profession, they would have been better satisfied with my decisions than the most of the regular profession placed thereon. Unlearned in those technical quibbles and specious sophisms, so much resorted to by the larger portion of the judiciary and lawyer-fraternity, to crush down the right and uphold the wrong, and ever adoring truth and justice, I would have sought to give practical illustration, in my official rulings, of the old English apothegm, that—"An upright Judge is a poor man's counsel." Alas! how few judges in most portions of this confederation of sovereign States, have won for themselves, of late years, such a proud distinction. With constant proclivity to decide in favor of grasping corporations, land monopolists, franchise grabbers, bankers, merchants and other robbers of the productive gains of society, these judges are ever seeking some book authority that they may, through strained or perverted construction of the mere letter of the law, justify their wrong renditions in favor of such depredators.

Among the illustrious jurists I would have taken for my model, is Chief Justice Marshall. Though not so learned in the law as he was, I should have followed his example in first finding out which party had the equity in such cases as may have come before me, and then hunting up or getting my colleagues, who agreed with me, to hunt up the law to sustain that side, which law can always be found. I should, likewise, have further followed the example of this wise and pure expounder of the law, by refusing to remand a case, on motion of any technical-mongering, hair-splitting and flaw-detecting attorney, because of some laches in the pleadings, defects of record, verbal inaccuracies or non-conformity to Court rules and regulations where no party could be injured, by then and there correcting such defects.

What vast injury, to many suitors, results from the contrary action of so many of our judges, whose wilful intent to wrong the party in the right, or actuated by that narrow pettifogging order of intellect, possessed by so many on the Bench, impel them to adhere to the strict letter. of its. law which killeth, and lose sight of the saving grace of its spirit.

I never filled but one official station, and that a judicial. In 1845 the Legislature of the " Provisional Government of Oregon," against my earnest protestation, elected me a District Judge of that outside and disputed Territory. I told them I was unqualified for the position, having never read a page of law. and moreover, would depart for California in a few months. But they said I was better fitted for a Judge than any of the few attorneys there. I presume they thought from the reputation I had established, in a two years residence among them, that I was a sort of natural born lawyer, and that judicial acumen grew in me like grains in wood. Consequently they took me from my log cabin, in the junction of the Clackamus and Willamette, where I lived alone, cultivating a few acres of grain, cabbage and potatoes, making shingles and catching salmon, to seat me on the figurative woolsack.

For thirty years the judges of California have, as a rule, strained the law to construe it in favor of the wrong. I should, as a judge, have strained it, somewhat, to maintain the right. Additional to the many misrulings of these recreant judges, mark their long delayed decisions, which was usually done to subserve the swindling purposes of monopolists, speculators and other law-shielded robbers.

The attorneys of this State, as well as the general public, believe these allegations to be true. Such attorneys well know that less their knowledge of the law, than other considerations, induces suitors to employ them. The stereotyped question of the most of such suitors, in important cases, when seeking counsel, has been—"How do you stand with the judge?" And the effort to stand well with their honors has rendered the Bar of California, especially here in San Francisco, the most servile and sycophantic in Christendom. However rank the offenses of these judges, however corrupt or incapable they may be, you will not hear of an attorney daring to brave their displeasure by criticising their conduct, much less, as is their duty, taking steps to bring them to trial and to judgment for their many offenses. Numbers of these attorneys have whispered in my ears—enjoining me not to mention their names— that they fully coincided with me as to the dishonesty or the incapacity of certain judges, especially that polluted pentarchy of the Supreme Bench. They have said to me that the whole of the present Court ought to be impeached for that one offence alone : the collusion and conspiracy which placed Wallace in the seat of the Chief Justice six years in advance of his legal turn, and has kept Crockett and Niles upon the bench after their legal terms had expired. But, said they to me, had any of us sought to arraign them on impeachment, or moved in Court to inquire into such usurpation, or even spoken loudly against them, in private, their vengeance would have been visited upon us as it has been upon you. They would have marred our cases before them, or hurt us in other courts. Our clients would have left us, and others been deterred from employing us.

Thus has a Jeffreys-like terrorum been exercised over the State by these notoriously corrupt and tyrannical instruments of a worse than kingly despot—the Money Monarchs of America.

Not in this discourse can I unfold the horrible persecutions I was subjected to, for eight months and a half, in the filthy bastile of San Francisco, for daring to take a step (the only one in my power) to arraign the traitorous conspirators sitting upon and defiling that tribunal, for their *own* gross contempt of the dignity, authority and majesty of the people. I did what I deemed a lofty duty. A duty which had no money valuation, since a million dollars would not have induced me to undergo such cruel torture. Any day I could have been released from it had I consented to utter but three words—to say to my imprisoners—*I did wrong.* I endured such torture for the sake of principle, and because my body only was imprisoned—my spirit was free and my conscience clear.

This cringing servility of the Bar which has estopped every member of it from denouncing the numerous blunders and criminal acts of these Supreme Justices, especially, the highhanded usurpation mentioned, and the severe vindictive and lawless punishment of myself for daring to better expose the same and striving to indirectly bring *them* to trial and to punishment, is, of itself, evidence of their guilt. In further attestation of such revengeful malice and guilt, permit me to relate two interesting incidents.

1. One of my attorneys in a suit for a large realty, in this city, pledged me to cease my strictures on the Supreme Court Justices after I had taken the suit, on appeal to them, as he

said it would ensure my defeat. I did then cease, but another writer continued to severely assail them through the papers, whose articles were, by the Court and by my counsel, imputed to my pen. Their decision was against me, when my attorney berated me in a passionate and insulting manner for violating my pledge to him, which he alleged had lost us the suit. I responded, that such a reflection upon their honors was as bad, or worse, than anything I had written about them. This shows the estimate in which they are held by their brother lawyers. I must, however, remark that prejudiced and revengeful as are these judicial rascals, they did not decide said suit against me on that ground. Property, in the city, to the value of several millions of dollars, mostly held adversely by the plundercrats, was involved in the issue, and heavy *douceurs* in the way of grand cash induced those venal judges to violate law, equity, and evidence, and decide as they did. This will all be proven when a new and unstocked deal of cards shall be had.

2. After I had been sent to prison for seating myself in the chair of bogus justice Crockett, on the 6th of August, 1874, in which I but followed his example set the first of January previous—by squatting in that seat against the express letter of the Constitution and statutes, the uniform usage in the premises and without popular authority, or the expressed permission of the judges, rightfully there—this same bogus justice admitted (at least, his son said it for him), that the severe penalty the Court had inflicted on me, was not so much for that mad freak of mine, as he termed it, but that I and others having so frequently, wrongfully, and roughly assailed them through the public prints, they had determined, whenever they got the opportunity, to make us smart for the same.

Whilst adducing incidents to illustrate my theme, I will call attention to a case alluded to by Kearney, in his late Salinas city speech, in which he spoke of that notorious land thief and congressional, legislative, judicial and land officials briber—Jesse D. Carr. Carr agreed to deed an interest in his Gabilan grant to a lawyer to assist him in securing a patent for it. He won the case and got the patent but refused to pay the lawyer. The latter sued him when Carr swore in open court that his title was a forgery and had been secured through fraud. Upon this showing he defeated the lawyer, has kept the land and remains outside the walls of the penitentiary. And such is law in California.

Another incident, a new Bar Association has just been formed in San Francisco. A member objected to one of the signers of the call to organize it, because he was an ex-convict from the East. Now, it was not the unfortunate fellow's crime they cared about, but any lawyer who could not keep out of the penitentiary, was held to be too big a fool to associate with the fraternity. They could condone the crime but not forgive the discovery or punishment. And of such are California lawyers, in the main.

Daniel O'Connell said that a cunning lawyer could drive a coach and four through any Act of Parliament, with a conniving or accommodating judge upon the Bench. But we have constantly witnessed the steaming of great railroad trains through and over our constitution and statute laws, by reason of this accommodating or conniving character of the judges.

We want a widely different order of judges, from the most of those California has been cursed with, especially on that foully tainted tribunal, the Supreme Court. I believe that should the Constitution be adopted, enough able and conscientious lawyers can be found to fill that Bench. For instance, there is that distinguished scholar and lawyer and most honorable gentleman, General Volney E. Howard. How will he do for Chief Justice ?

And associated with him, those two able and impartial jurists, as proven by their records, Nathaniel Bennett and David S. Terry. With such men as these upon that long defiled tribunal, we shall have less JUGGLERY, JARGON and INJUSTICE, and more sound sense, pure law and justice.

One of the plundercratic organs of this city, the *Post*, contained, the other day, a pyramidal arrangement of the names of certain well-known citizens, mine among them, which were

satirically termed, " Fossil Remains," and surmised, by the
editor, to have belonged to the Silurian epoch, which remains
purported to have been recently dug up in Tulare. So far as
concerns myself, I admit that I have been, virtually, buried
this quarter of a century, beneath the diluvial *debris* of
fraud, robbery, corruption and every species of wrong with
which these workers of iniquity have covered this lovely west-
ern land. Is it not time the people of California had exhumed
such fossils, whether found in the Silurian or other of the Pal-
eozoic ages, and restored them to their once influential positions ?

The unprogressive condition of the minds of the most of our
judges and lawyers has been exemplified by their adherence to
certain old English common law ideas, as to land tenures, water
privileges, mining rights and other obsolete, or to us, inapplic-
able legal constructions. That was a most palpably false decision made by the U. S. Supreme Court, which holds, that the
precious metals, in Spanish grants, belong to the proprietors of
such grants. This is contrary to equity, as well as to the laws
of Spain and Mexico, from whence these land grants were derived. Thus old Feudalic and Bourbonic king-governed Spain
discountenances this monopoly of such minerals, as well as
water, which Republican America sanctions. The most con-
clusive arguments penned, some years ago, against such misconstruction of mining rights, were by two laymen or non-professional lawyers, George Gordon and myself. Gordon published an able pamphlet on the question, and I, some newspaper
articles. This false decision was rendered regarding the famous Fremont Mariposa grant of ten square leagues. Among the
other judicially indorsed rascalities of this grant, was to permit
the location to be so altered from where it had been located
and surveyed by the claimants, prior to the gold discovery, as
to touch not one foot of the land included in the boundaries
originally marked out. It was taken up bodily from the
lowlands, and set down in the foot-hills of the Sierra, in order to
cover a gold-bearing region. This decision was then so ordered
by the great banking and speculating firm of Palmer, Cook &

Co., which, for several years, absolutely ruled all California, and wielded a powerful influence at Washington. Joe Palmer would have been appointed Secretary of the Treasury, provided, that compound of knave and fool, John C. Fremont, had been elected President of the U. S. in 1856.

The Federal Supreme Court—following a previously enunciated judgment by the Supreme Court of California—also, rendered a shamefully false decision in " Whitney *vs.* Frisbie," which proclaimed the doctrine that a pre-emptioner of the public domain acquired no right nor title to his land until receiving a patent therefor ; and that Congress could, at any time, before the issuance of such patent, take his claim from him and give or sell it to another. And even, in some instances, a patent has not protected him, since Congress and the Courts have, subsequently, held that certain railroad bonus grants took precedence of such patents.

The fruits of this infamous and most damnable decision have been to drive from their homesteads, in various States and Territories, thousands of settlers—many such homesteads long lived upon and highly improved—and title to the same vested in railway incorporators and other favored monopolists. In fact, the primary tenure of our Public Lands has been misconstrued by both Congress and the Courts ; and, per consequence, millions on millions of acres of this common mon estate of the people — of this *cestui que* property — have been swindled into the hands of speculating monopolists, through the assistance of such faithless trustees.

During several years I have been urging, in some of my pamphlets, and otherwise, that the settlers on the public lands should *arm* themselves and defend, by force, their homesteads against these legalised despoilers. In some isolated instances they have done so, but meeting with so little sympathy or active support from others of their fellow-citizens, they have been compelled to acquiesce in such spoliation. But the times, thank God ! are ripening for a different result.

The settlers in the upper Tulare Valley have recently formed military companies to defend their homes against the rapacity of cormorant claimants of their land. Success of the Workingmen's Party will, ultimately, ensure them victory.

Let them stand to their guns, bide their time and vote the right ticket.

We want men sent to Congress and the Legislature and placed upon our high Court benches who will reverse all this wrong-doing and restore these stolen acres to such estate, to be properly parceled out and possessed.

This doctrine I have been proclaiming over twenty years, yet have been unheeded. But now that these lands of value have all been thus gobbled up by speculators, and homeless millions—defrauded of a due share in this heritage of all—are beginning to open their eyes to such fact, we may look for some speedy rectification of such great wrong.

Relevantly, I may mention here a just decision, of vast importance, recently rendered by the Hon. Philip Keyser, Judge of the 10th Judicial District. It was the granting of a perpetual injunction against the operation of certain hydraulic miners, the *debris* from whose mines have been washed down upon large areas of agricultural lands of the Sacramento valley and destroyed their fertility. Such decision was not alone demanded to guard from further injury the rights of individual owners of these lands, but the paramount interest of the entire community requires that such arable acres shall not be thus destroyed. Should no other remedy be devised to prevent this, then ought such mining to be prohibited. Protection of such soil is a duty of the State. We can do without gold and silver (fiat paper money may be substituted), but not without bread and meat.

Kearney's fierce and fearless assailment of the "Court House rings" and corrupt domination of large landed proprietors in the southern counties, prompts me to mention my efforts to expose the same during a trip made through, and a stay in those counties in the years 1868–9. I then sent several communications, as a regular correspondent, to the *Alta California*, and a few to the *Examiner*. Neither paper would publish what I stated about the corrupt practices of certain Supervisors and Assessors down that way. Remaining in Los Angeles near three months, I got full and exact information as to various offenses of these and other officials of that county, as well as of certain large landholders there. In one of my letters to the *Examiner* I cited the fact that, additional to their manufactur ing a Pueblo title and then stealing the land (as the same sort of rascals did the "Pueblo" of San Francisco), the owners of several large ranchos, in such vicinity, had been selling off small tracts to farmers at ten dollars per acre; that after this was done, along came the Assessor (a tool of these grant holders), who not only assessed such small holdings at what had been paid for them, but the improvements placed thereon, farming implements, working cattle and growing crops; and at the same time assessed the like quality of land, yet remaining in the hands of the grant holders, at one dollar per acre. I contended in that letter, as have often done before and since, that improved lands should be assessed at no higher rates than unimproved of the same quality, and that growing crops and farming implements should be exempt.

Among the excellent features of the newly drafted Constitution, growing crops are exempted, and all lands of equal natural fertility assessed alike. If any discrimination were made, a premium should be given the cultivator, by assessing his land at a less rate.

That letter to the *Examiner* was not published. On my return to San Francisco, I inquired of Mr. Geo. Pen Johnston, managing editor, whether he had received it? He had. Did he believe I had given any false information in it? He said, he doubted not I had related only the truth. Then why, I further queried, did you not print it? Because, replied he, Los Angeles is a good Democratic county, and I did not wish to assail our friends there.* And this is precisely what both Democratic and Republican party organs and politicians have always done, and are now doing—condoning, covering up or defending the worst rascality in their respective ranks. And yet a lot of fools, belonging to each, pretend to look for reforms in and from such parties.

Since its organization the protesting cry of the interior has

---

* How about that Democratic county now?

been—that San Francisco selfishly and dishonestly ruled the State—that the toll-gatherers, middlemen, merchants and money lenders at the Golden Gate not alone extorted and monopolised all the profits of their labor, as well as evaded paying their just taxation, but corrupted their rural representatives in the legislature and other officials. These allegations are well founded. But, at length, the long beduped and manipulated voters of San Francisco, who were made the instruments to maintain this corrupt and corrupting dynasty, have revolted against it and called on the interior population to join them in rescuing the entire State from the throat-grasp of these robbers. Are they responding to this call ? Or, will they, serf-like, and ass-like, permit themselves to be bamboozled to a different action by their Court-house rings of office-holders, professional politicians, lawyers, merchants, and local newspapers, all of whom are in league with the great plunder rings of San Francisco and the State capital.*

The recent great shrinkage in the values of property, will, under the old Constitution and rule of the present order of officials, cause an increase in taxation; but let the new Constitution be adopted, which will ensure the election of a new character of officials, when taxation will be greatly reduced, because of the hundreds of millions more of property which will then be assessed that have hitherto escaped. The holders of this large amount of property—mostly belonging to San Francisco, are, of course, strenuously opposed to the new Constitution.

I will read to you, as apropos to my general subject, some extracts from a pamphlet published—" *Address to the California Legislature.*" It is dated Sacramento, March 1st, 1874. That, you may remember, was the " Dolly Varden " Legislature, the perhaps, honestest set of Assemblymen—that is, the major portion of them—we have had in California, but the greatest band of asses. We then sent from this city to the Assembly, four loud talking Dolly Varden Reformers ! who

---

* Having strong belief that the interior would affirmatively respond I made several small bets upon the general result. I expected, however, a larger majority than was given.

being, in fact, cunning, deep-scheming, mealy-mouthed and
treacherous politicians and lawyers, soon got those Dolly
Varden asses from the interior, harnessed up, when, taking the
reins, they drove them to suit their purposes, throughout that
session. These asses brayed, kicked, pulled, backed or stood
still, just as those rascally drivers directed; and four grander
scamps than they never crossed the threshold of that Assembly Chamber. Their names are, M. M. Estee, who was made
Speaker, J. F. Cowdery, D. Freidenrich and John F. Swift.
Estee and Swift had more brains but less principle than the
others, provided anything like principle could be found among
the quartette. Swift's record before and since that period, as a
deep-scheming demagogue and money-making mountebank,
bears the palm over most any such tide-floating bamboozlers
of the inane populace that California has produced, prolific of
such genus as this mongrel muck heap of humanity has been.
Swift has often said to me that he despises the populace, and
only uses them for his selfish ends. He thus used the voters
of his district in 1877, to send him to the Legislature for the
sole purpose of securing payment of his swindling $30,000
water suit fee against this city; and, also, to insiduously prevent
the passage of any law that would deprive the Spring Valley
Water Company of their swindling monopoly.

In truth, all these trafficing politicians—especially those in
the Democratic ranks—entertain intense hatred towards the
common multitude. This arises from the fact that they, in
order to curry favor and win popularity, demean themselves
by doing and uttering so many things they believe to be un-
dignified and false, that, mortified at having to stoop so low to
conquer, they, by a natural revulsion, become enraged at such
instruments of their selfish ambition for compelling them to
thus act. This feeling is further attested by the quickness
with which those elected to office violate their pledges and
spurn the ladder on which they climbed to eminence. And
we now witness still further evidence of the same in the bitter
denunciations daily hurled by nearly all the old Democratic
politicians in the city, and perhaps in other portions of the
State, against the rank and file, and their newly chosen leaders,
of such faith, because they will no longer be led by such renegade pretenders, and refuse to again put them in office.

This same political somersaulter and tide-waiter Swift, as well as other notorious tricksters of the two old parties of the Bob Ferral and M. M. Estee stripe, are now resorting to all sorts of insidious secret manœuvers and open demagogic arts to ingratiate themselves with the new party in order to secure nominations to office, else humbug its leaders into supporting some rascally scheme of the plundercrats, in whose employ they are. Spring Valley Water Company Swift (he has all along been a secret agent of theirs though ostensibly opposing them) as yet keeps one foot on the piebald Republican steed, whilst little Bob, the Artful Dodger, has a foot on the wind-broken, stringhalted and spavined Democratic.

Swift and Pixley are *sub rosa* partners in various schemes of villainy. Both are in the pay and service of the Central Pacific Railroad Company, Spring Valley Water Company and other monopolies. Whilst Pixley runs his *Argonaut* in support of these corporations, and viciously denounces Kearney and the Workingmen's Party, Swift is privately and treacherously striving through artful blarney and humbuggery, to deceive Kearney and other leaders of such party, in order to exercise an evil influence over them and it, divert such party from the great reform movement it has marked out for its mission, and render it subservient to the purposes of the plundercrats.

I presented a petition that session for the impeachment of the judges of the Supreme Court, reciting in it certain high crimes and misdemeanors of which they were accused, but the four sham "reformers!" mentioned, supported by all the other lawyers in the Assembly, stopped its reading, raised a great hubbub in the Chamber over it, and ended by inducing Speaker Estee to violate my constitutionally guaranteed right of petition, as well as violate all parliamentary proceedings, in arbitrarily ruling it out of order and directing the document to be returned to the author.

It was from witnessing the Machiavellian scheming and lawless action in that Legislature of these four agents of the plunderocracy, and the artful and dishonest manipulations and jesuitical jugglery of lawyers in preceding ones and elsewhere,

as well as my general reading, which prompted me to pen
such a severe stricture upon that class, as will be found in the
"Address." I make a more extended allusion to such Legislature for another reason—that it is often cited by those who
still adhere to the Democratic and Republican organizations,
as attesting the inutility of getting up any more new parties ;
and they prophecy that the Workingmen's Party, if successful
this year, will prove as shortlived and abortive as that Dolly
Varden. I have admitted it would—that is, under its existing
organization, if any more such assinines and knaves as were
wafted into that Legislature and other public places, on that
quickly upsurging and subsiding wave of popular opinion,
shall be chosen by the existing new party.

A great disadvantage the Workingmen Party labors under,
is that nearly all its representative men (Kearney included) are
so little acquainted with our leading and lesser politicians, lawyers, writers, etc., and so little posted in the general and special
rascality practised, through many years, by these agents of the
plunderocracy, and at the same time are as unacquainted with
those who have always combated with such class. Hence, are
liable to be imposed upon by the beguilings of these agents,
and treacherous whisperings of those, in their own ranks, who
are in the secret service and pay of the plundercrats. Both
of these feed servitors are constantly laboring to popularise,
with the sincere Workingmen leaders and their rank and file, certain pretended friends, but, at heart, traitorous scamps, in order
to have them wield influence and secure nominations for office;
at the same time insidiously defaming men of high moral
worth and ability, who are heart and soul in sympathy with
their cause, in order to prejudice such party and its leaders
against them, and thus prevent their wielding any influence,
or receiving nominations for office.

But Kearney and his Sand Lot surroundings are not alone
thus ignorant of who is who in California. How few among
this heterogeneous conglomeration of gold-seekers, so suddenly
maelstromed into such beautiful virgin ravished demesne have
proved themselves the wiser ? Have not all alike unrecognized
the wise and virtuous among them, and filled, with rare exceptions, their public posts with the unwise and unvirtuous ? There

is one class who have fully recognized both orders—the bad and the good. These are the leading plundercrats, who, seeking instruments to serve their villainous purposes, have tempted and tested every prominent man of intellect in the State. *They* know the venal, because they have bribed and used them; and they know whom they have failed to bribe and use.

Therefore, onward let this revolution roll. Good will come of it. The virtuous and the highly intellectual all favor it, because they perceive that through such, lies the only road to reformation. The fear, as said, entertained by many, that a greater amount of incompetency will be wafted into public places on this rising popular floodwave, may be well founded. History, which is ever repeating itself, teaches such fact. But these incompetents and unvirtuous cannot long maintain position and will give place to the wisest and the best. The country has long been under the rule of incompetents and knaves, of presumptuous and successful mediocrity. The time is approximating when its men of genius and heroic virtue will be placed at the helm of affairs. A storm is brewing, and when the tempest shall howl and dangerously toss the ship of state, this order of pilots and commanders will be called for. These can only be recognized and exalted by the, then, mad-passioned and affrighted multitude, through this upheaval of society.

Let Kearney and his party continue to agitate, since through agitation comes rectification. They are, I repeat, performing their allotted task. Let us give all due credit to them. But let me say this to Denis Kearney—that if he would, like Garibaldi—Italy's great commoner agitator—continue to wield influence, he must follow Garibaldi's example, by continuing to menace the foundations of the Government, unless the ablest and most virtuous men of the State' are placed in position to effect the demanded reforms. And let him—waiving place himself, as he says he will—assist in selecting such, instead of the incompetents he has hitherto been supporting for public stations. He did not create the Workingmen's party, as the plundercrats declare, since it is not in the power of any man or set of men to create a party. This Kearney himself has often told them, which proves he has more brains than they. He must, however, soon rid himself of two orders of bad advisers—the ignoramus and treacherous comrades in his own class, and that small squad of shyster lawyers who, accidentally getting into prominence in his party, are much misleading him with their false counsel.

The portents on every hand presage an approximating social and political upheaval of a very menacing character throughout our American land. A vindicatory spirit is pervading the mass, who more and more fiercely demand that juster laws shall be enacted and more impartially administered, or wo to those who shall prevent such.

Hence, in event the new Constitution shall be adopted, there are four primarily important places to be filled with men of upright character, high intelligence and stern resolve—the Gubernatorial, Legislative, Railroad Commission and Supreme Judicial. Should the to be newly chosen Justices of this high Court be of that better type I have portrayed ; should they earnestly strive to estop that law-protected exploitation, by the preying portion of society (its cunning and all-grasping nonproducers), of the wealth evolved by the great army of producers, then will be appeased this justly incensed and revolutionary threatening multitude. Then will they estop the growth of communistic ideas, and reconcile the conflicting interests of classes. It will give again supremacy to moral forces, which should, mainly, be relied on to preserve order and secure the enforcement of just laws.

But who are the Communists among us ? If Communism means dishonorably appropriating, through the forms of prostituted law, the property of others—of thus monopolizing the wealth of the country—then are these plundercrats, who have been ruling and robbing the State from its beginning, the real Communists. They allege that the Kearneyites, so-called, want to get into power to steal. *They* have already been stealing. The one may become rogues. The others are.

My countrymen, I desire to impress upon you this serious admonition, this most earnest injunction—that in selecting Supreme Judges, the Governor, Legislators and Railroad Commissioners, you have need to not alone secure ordinarily honest and sensible men, but brave men—men of heroic courage—men of lofty souls—men of high moral nerve—men who wor-

3

ship truth—men who cleave, through good and evil report, to principle—men who always place their cause in advance of self—men of clear and positive convictions—men who will dare and do—men who will perform their duty regardless of what may occur. Those of mere honesty and intelligence may be easily found, if earnestly sought, since we have numbers of them ; but men possessing those other traits, without which these latter are of little service in such positions, are extremely rare.

You ask me how such shall be discerned. My answer is, study well the antecedents of a suggested candidate. Find out whether any stigma sullies his escutcheon. Learn whether he has been much and often tried by great temptations and afflictions, and has withstood these trials. Such are the only safe criterions to judge by.

The horrible revelations of crime which will be made when the Workingmen's Party representatives shall be everywhere installed in office in the State—provided they be of the order described—will astound the world.

Thirty years villainy of unparalleled atrocity, will then be exposed, and, as far as possible, punished. To prevent this, every desperate expedient will be resorted to by the corrupt old politicians of the Democratic and Republican parties to keep one or the other in power, that the plundercratic dynasty, to which they hold leal allegiance, may be maintained. These politicians are now engaged issuing their lying, hypocritical and bamboozling pronunciamentos in order to stem the enrolling revolution. They and their plundercratic employers begin to perceive the terrorizing handwriting on the wall, and trembling with the cowardice of a guilty conscience, will, to their already innumerable crimes, add new ones to save themselves from loss of power and consequent exposure and punishment. Why should any voter in California, unless a participant in their crimes, a recipient of their booty and bounty, or an incorrigible fool, assist to uphold the longer this villainous and most ruinous power ?

I largely favor this new Constitution and its inevitable results, because its adoption will be a peaceable revolution ; whereas, its rejection, by keeping in power a portion of the existing rulers and their policy, would, inevitably, inaugurate a chaotic bloody revolution ere long.

If the present propitious period to emancipate themselves from the accursed thraldom of the Money Power and its minions and allies—the lawyers, preachers, journalists and professional politicians—be not availed of, I know not when or how such slavish people can be incited to legitimate peaceable action again. If so judicially blinded to their own interests, so demented and maddened, it must be that the gods have doomed them to destruction.

It is useless to talk about having more than two parties in California this year, or the next either. The great, the paramount, the all controling issue is between those who sustain the existing plundercratic dynasty and those seeking to overthrow it. Upon this line of demarcation let every one select his side.

These plundercratic villains failing to demoralize, dissever and break up the Workingmen's organization, by the unlawful, tyrannical and infamous measures hitherto resorted to by them, are now engaged in a new role of rascality to effect their diabolic purposes. Among these new devices is to hypocritically echo one of the tocsin cries of the Workingmen's Party—"The Chinese must go!" This is all a sham upon their part, and alone intended to divert voters from the vital issues of the campaign. They have, likewise, purchased several prominent members of the Workingmen's Party and will purchase more, in order to sow seeds of discord and breed doubt and disaffection in its ranks. They will strive to have men of bad records put up by it for office, that such records may be exposed, and the party thuswise injured and such candidates defeated. And they will inspire their hireling newspapers to defame other nominees, though such should be as wise and pure as Washington. To counteract the influence of this address and depopularise its author, these scoundrels will, doubtless, search my published writings (not daring to assail me otherwise) of the past third of a century, to find some speculative theory, or satirical or angered expression that may be warped to offend some in the party I have long labored to have organized, or prevent others from joining it.

Additional to their bribe money already expended in subsidizing newspapers, buying up saleable leaders or prominent
speakers of the Workingmen's Party, and bamboozling money
outlayed for rent of large halls, paying for music and advertise-
ments of meetings held in them—called in the name of Democratic, Republican and " Central Club Workingmen's " organizations—these wealthy plundercrats are disbursing vast sums
in sending out many other speakers, (several of them heavily
feed lawyers) and flooding the State with innumerable lying
documents opposed to the adoption of the New Constitution ;
whilst additional large sums will be used to corrupt public
officers and purchase votes to secure a dishonest result through
the ballot box, whether in the plébiscitum to be given on the
Constitution or that, subsequently, cast for candidates.

It is most palpable that nearly all the false constructions,
of many portions of the New Constitution, and bitter opposition
to its adoption, on the part of the plundercrats and their
pensioned servitors, arises not because of any fears of its hurtful operation, of itself, but that if adopted, the same decree
will auspicate the triumph and future rule of the Workingmen's,
or, some similar party, in California.

This, the real reason of their opposition, has been admitted
by many of them.   That once high-toned and excellent paper,
but now miserable, degraded bawd—the San Francisco *Examiner*—which has sold its virtue and gone a-whoring with the
Central Pacific Railroad Grandees and their confrere plundercrats—has publicly proclaimed this to be the paramount incen-
tive for its opposing the New Constitution.   The *Examiner*, as
well as nearly all the leading politicians of California, belonging to the Democratic Party, or rather, the late Democratic
Party here, have bartered their honor and their patriotism to
the plundercrats, during the past several years, chiefly through
the pandering instrumentality of that Railroad Company's
political pimp or twin procurer-general—Doctor Wm. M.
Gwin.   He and W. W. Stow—*par nobile fratrum*—are Emperor Stanford's mediums for buying up every one venal whom
that potentate may have dishonest use for.   Stanford and the
other plundercrats have subsidized, *douceured* or bribed about
three-fourths of the newspapers of the State to oppose the
New Constitution.

This vile instrument Stow, has disbursed for the Central
Pacific Railroad Company, alone, during the past dozen years,
to purchase governors, legislators, judges and other public
functionaries ; to pay lobbyists, lawyers and subsidized newspapers, not less than three millions of dollars. The people's
own money, extorted and stolen from them with which to
bribe their public servants and pollute their laws ! And he is
now financial manager of the " Literary Bureau " of the plundercrats in this city, disbursing the immense sum contributed by
the bankers, merchants, stock gamblers, large land grabbers
and others, to defeat the New Constitution.

Speaking of the *Examiner*, this paper is terribly exercised
over two recent communications, of marked ability, emanating
from Democratic pens ; the one signed " Orantes," which, its
proprietors were compelled to admit in its own columns; the
other signed " Woodchopper," which appeared in the Colusa
Sun, the leading interior Democratic paper, and like the *Examiner*, bought up by the plundercrats to oppose the New Constitution.

These correspondents tore the mask from the face of this lying, hypocritical and subsidized " leading Democratic paper of
the State." They exposed its recreancy to principle, its abjura-
tion of every tenet of its party's faith, its false and vindictive
assailment of Denis Kearney, and insults heaped upon the old
rank and file of the Democratic party, because they chose to be
no longer gulled by the *Examiner* and its gang of time-serving
dishonest professional politicians, headed by Governor Irwin,
U. S. Senator Farley and Doctor Gwin.

And to further attest the genuine animus actuating these
plundercratic cormorants, vultures, hawks, jackdaws, spiders,
hyenas and coyotes; that it is not the merits or demerits of the
New Constitution they care one fig about, or know anything
about—it is a fact that not one in fifty of them has read a line
of it. I listened last week to one of these capitalists berating
Judge Pratt for sustaining the New Constitution, who declared
that a man of his fine intellect and large wealth, must be mad
to advocate the adoption of that sand lot, hoodlum and communistic document. Said Pratt to him, I have read and re-read
every line in it, and regard it as an excellent Constitution, with

some defects, of course; but will you please point out what particular features are so obnoxious to you ? And what was the response of this indignant Moneybag—Sir, I have not read a line of the infernal thing, and do not intend to read it.

It is threatened that capital (cash capital) will leave the State in the event of the adoption of this Organic Act. Now, if we can rid the community of many of these Capitalists, it will be greatly to our advantage, even should they take such money capital with them ; since, in place of it, there will be augmented a certain character of capital we greatly more require than gold and silver. It is the creation and active employment of sentiments of honor, truth and patriotism—of fidelity to public and to private trusts. This is the character of capital we have the greatest need of; and it is these identical money-grasping Shylocks who, chiefly, prevent the fructification, cultivation and utilization of such indispensable capital and currency. Let these Plundercrats go !

The objections made by the plundercratic organs to certain alleged defects of the new Constitution are frivolous, false, carping, hypercritical and hypocritical. In truth, it is not the character of this proposed Organic Act that these plundercrats and their servitors so much object to, as said before, as the dread of the Workingmen electing their many candidates and taking possession of the State and city governments, in the event it shall be adopted by the people. This is what strikes terror to their guilty souls. What care these men about any sort of Constitution as long as they can fill the offices with their creatures ? Can they not then ignore the new as well as they have the old ?

They and their mercenary speakers and penmen contend that the old Constitution should be maintained, because the Courts have been for thirty years construing and settling its provisions; and that to adopt the new will tend to unsettle such questions and decisions. Now, whatever has been righteously determined will remain, even should the new be substituted ; but what these thieves so greatly dread is, that these thirty years of misconstruction or ignoration of the old Constitution and statute laws will be set aside, under a new Organic Act, just statutes made in conformity therewith, and properly construed

by honorable and intelligent judges, and they be made to disgorge the vast booty acquired through those long years of
legalized spoliation. These depredators deprecate the popular
threat of "cinching capitalists." Now, since the most of these
capitalists have been cinching the people these many years, is
it not time the tables were turned ?

I have stated elsewhere in this discourse, that these plundercrats not only seek to have no obstacles placed in the way of
their thieving schemes, but prevent investigation of the numerous crimes of which they are guilty. For instance, that one
alone—the bribery of Assessor Rosener of San Francisso
county, wherein at least two hundred of our, so called, "leading, wealthiest and best" citizens, including bankers and other
money-lenders, big merchants, ship-owners, and large real
estate holders, can be proved guilty and sent to the penitentiary for from one to fourteen years. The Grand Juries, Courts
and Prosecuting Attorneys have all been bribed during the
past five years to prevent these criminals from being indicted,
tried, convicted and punished. No wonder these fellows are
shelling out their cash so liberally to defeat the Constitution
and Workingmen's party, with the State prison doors thus
staring them in the face.

Wm. C. Ralston, Cashier of the Bank of California, was
treasurer of this bribery fund, and kept a list of all contribu-
tors to it. That list is, no doubt, in the possession of Wm.
Sharon or D. O. Mills. When the time shall have arrived to
demand it, a *thumbscrew*, if nothing short, will produce it.

Another manouver of these plundercrats and their cunning
henchmen, to divert attention from their crimes and the great
and vital issues of the State, is to interject general or Federal
politics. Except the Chinese, no such questions should, this
year, be listened to or spoken about here by any having the
welfare of California at heart. Discussion of the proposed
new Constitution and other local measures, and selection of
proper men to effect these home reforms, should alone engross
our attention at present.

What arrant hypocracy for all these, at heart, pro-Chinese
and land monopoly papers and politicians, to cry out against
the new Constitution, because Chinese immigration and land

monopoly have not been expressly prohibited in it. Had such clauses been inserted, these same papers and politicians would have denounced them. A notorious agent of the plundercrats, in the Convention (Col. Barnes), did, jesuitically and hypocritically, strive to have engrafted an obnoxious Chinese Article for this very purpose. He and other such agents in that body and out of it—disciples of the anti-State Rights and "Universal Brotherhood of Man" school—went back on all their teachings of such tenets, to more fiercely than any denounce the Chinese, and proclaim the most ultra State Sovereignty doctrine. But who so gullible as to believe them sincere?

Among the complicated and Janus-faced contradictions and hypocricies of some of the opponents of the new Constitution, is the outcry of all the Railroad organs against the Railroad Commission, provided for in such instrument. They object to it because, they say. that three men can be more easily bribed by Stanford & Co., (their own masters), than can one hundred Legislators. Why do not these unartful dodgers place the question rightly before their readers? Why do they not tell them that the fully tried experiment in California, and many Eastern States, has demonstrated the utter inability of a Legislature to manage railway matters—that these can alone be done by a Commission, and that the only question is, shall the Legislature or the People elect the Commissioners. The present Constitution permits the Legislature to elect them, the submitted new one, authorizes the people, directly, to do it. Two of king Stanford's oily-tongued servitors Creed Haymond and A. A. Cohen, are making speeches to prove that the Railroad Commission scheme was concocted in Convention through the secret artifices of the Railroad Company, and hence, their virtuous opposition to the new Constitution. Oh! I used to have a good opinion of the intellect, though never any faith in the honesty of these two men. But after manifesting such assininity as to imagine they can gull a single voter, in the State, with this barefaced bamboozlery, I cease to have such opinion of their sense.

The same hypocritical inconsistency, however, marks the

conduct of all the other Railroad Company's servitors, their newspaper organs included, who charge that this Commission is the very thing these Companies desire, yet vehemently oppose the adoption of the new Constitution.

They assert that three men cannot be found, in all California, whom these Railroad Companies will be unable to bribe. Doubtless, such cannot in their ranks.

The projected new Constitution compels the rich, who have, heretofore, evaded their proper taxation, to pay in full, and thus reduce the percentage of levy, and so benefit the man of small means, who has always been assessed at the full value of his property; yet these same rich fellows, voicing through their hireling mouthpieces, effect to believe that the instrument discriminates against the poor. What solicitude these wolves have for the welfare of the sheep !

But one of the best feature in all the new Constitution is that *section* which relegates to the respective counties the management of their local affairs. This is not only a sound republican feature of government, but removes from the Legislature that vast log-rolling corruption appliance (local and special legislation), which has been used by the great corporations and other plunderers, to carry their iniquitous measures through that body.

Home, or neighborhood, self-rule is the true conservation of liberty—the best safeguard against centralization and despotism. For years, the people of California have been demanding this change in our organic law so as to secure such natural right. It is guaranteed in the new Constitution, yet we find every solitary plundercratic organ in the State, opposing the clause. Wherefore ? Because it removes from the Legislative halls that corrupting leverage, the great corporations and political schemers have always relied on to further their rascally ends. It is a cardinal principle of the Democratic party's creed, yet, we find the *S. F. Examiner*, the leading organ of such party, in California, equally with the Republican leading organ—the Sacramento *Record-Union*—strongly opposing it.

There is only one paper in the State which has outlied the

Examiner in misconstruing the new Constitution, and that is its brother railroad organ, the *Record-Union.*

Another reason for the *Examiner's* false course lies in the fact that its founder and principle owner, is a wealthy, penurious, cent per-centing old Shylock.

The bulldosing movement of the land monopolists, bankers, merchants, stock gamblers, and others of their ilk, to inaugurate a panic and force a greater depression of prices and monetary stringency, to operate against the new Constitution, should the stronger induce all seeking good government to vote for it. When were these classes, in any country, ever known to favor just laws, and act the part of honest citizens ? In the language of the illustrious Napoleon—" Merchants have no honor, no patriotism, they will sell their country for a sous." And what says the great historian, Gibbon, about them—" Of all classes of a community the mercantile is the least patriotic and the most dishonest."

Mark the recent language of that generalisimo of the " Pick Pandle Brigade," representative merchant Coleman, who sneeringly termed the advocates of the New Constitution a " rabble," and declared that the country should not be governed by its ignorant or " unthinking majority."

This insolent, upstart trafficer, has blurted out the true inwardness of nearly all his class. It is because he and his kind have been ruling the entire country for forty years, that every sound, economic governmental idea has become perverted, and all the laws made and construed to crush the industrial or producing classes, and discriminate in favor of the non-producing trafficers, speculators and monopolists.

The time is close at hand when another Jackson will arise to throttle these long dictating and polluting bankers and merchants.

This *Bourgeoisie* component of society (residing in the towns and cities) have, everywhere, all over the State, antagonised themselves to the others by opposing the New Constitution; and in other portions of our country, actuated by the same selfish motives, as in Ancient Rome, modern France, Germany, in fact, all countries, manage to seize upon and control affairs, so

as to bring about those bloody internal convulsions, to which
their unbearable exploitations, oppressions and pollution, at
length drive the others to revolt against.

In all countries, and in every age, this *bourgeoisie* class has
been the incarnation of extreme selfishness, and, consequently,
the most dishonest element of society. They constitute the
worst *preying* portion of it, infinitely worse than the house bur-
glar, highway robber and petty thief, because the latter steal
outside the pale of the law, and in open defiance of it; whereas, the others pervert the law, and corrupt its makers and ad-
ministers, in order to steal inside its protecting pale. These
would have all the laws made for their especial benefit, and to
guard and unjustly add to their stores of wealth. They place
the protection of property of paramount importance to the protection of persons. The value of a man, in their estimation,
should be measured by what he extrinsically has, not by what
he intrinsically is. They have ever been the foes of the wise
and the virtuous, because the wise and the virtuous have ever,
of necessity, been antagonistic to their erroneous ideas and dishonest actings.

I have, for several years, as my numerous writings and much
talkings attested, essayed to have, as a *denier resort*, to correct
the deep and all-pervading evils afflicting the body politic,
short of a bloody revolution—towards which we are rapidly
drifting—just such an organization as this Workingmen's Part y
Of course, I do not indorse its phantasies and fallacies and uto-.
pian expectations, but these are inconsequential. History has
taught me that such social and political upheaval of the sub-
strata, was a pre-requisite to any reform, in such a condition
of society as ours.

The main object and effect of a victory to such new organization, will be to smash the machinery of the two rotten old parties, in this State; to deprive their professional and incurably
corrupt and selfish politicians and leaders of all influence, and
oust from office their venal and inefficient representatives. Th is
removes hitherto insurmountable obstacles to any reforms, a nd
opens the way for ulterior methods, and measures to secure s uch.

For it matters not how good a man is who may be placed in office by the Democratic or Republican Party, or any party ruled by the plunderocracy, he will achieve no reform, because the machinery of those effete and expiring old parties will so trammel and control him, as to render useless any efforts or desires he may have or take, in such direction. The camarilla or secret "power behind the throne," which controls the machine, will dictate his action.

For years, these parties have been alternately victorious in California, and the elect of each have vied as to which should do more harm instead of good to the country—which should more faithfully assist the plunderings of the plundercrats.

To the credit of the Democratic rank and file—that is, the great body of them—they have repudiated their faithless leaders and organized a new party.

The Workingmen's party is the true Democratic party of the State ; because it is the only party of progress, the party of reform, the party of the people, and the only party opposed to the infernal rule of the plunderocracy.

Dray-driver Kearney, its present recognized leader, is an iconoclast—a rough breaker of false political images, which have so long been worshiped by a bigoted, suicidal and deluded populace. He is engaged in a legitimate undertaking—tearing down the rotten structures of the body politic. As he and his surrounding aids know little about uprearing new ones, efficient architects must be sought and set to work to rebuild the better. Let Kearney and his kind pull down the old—let others uprear the new. Of course the former conceive themselves competent for both tasks, and will essay to solve the intricate problems of government, or, alone, select the men to do it. Kearney says we must choose for office (law-makers included) dray-drivers, stevedores, bricklayers, mechanics, cooks, common laborers and the like—men of bone and brawn. But I would cite him to what Plato, in the *Republic*, dialogues about this. Says such illustrious philosopher : "If I build a city I employ carpenters and masons ; if a ship, shipwrights ; if a coach, wheelrights and other handiwork artificers or craftsmen, according to their especial callings. But to choose public Guardians—men to manage the affairs of State—I would select from that rare few only those fitted by nature and by education for such lofty and responsible duties."

There can be no legitimate objection to men of strong muscle and from the manual labor ranks being selected as such Guardians, provided they have the best brain capacity and other superior fitness to fill such stations. "Knowledge is power." It is brain, not brawn, which rules the world.

Were our artisans and common labor classes as virtuous and enlightened as were the plebeians or common people of Rome, at the establishment of the Tribunitian system of government, and for centuries, subsequently, they would know whom to choose for office. But this need not be looked for until our entire people shall adopt a similar form of government—at least, a separate and concurrent class rule—to that most admirably checked and balanced one. And this must early come to pass, else through the throes of a terrible sanguinary conflict will come the mailed hand of Cæsar.

"History is philosophy teaching by example." Many have perused its pages, few have derived wisdom lessons therefrom; hence, the lettered as well as the unlettered grovel on in Cimmerian darkness, and become wiser only through sadful and dearbought experience. But the mother wit instincts and earlier suffering experiences of the unlettered masses, illuminate their intellects to a clearer conception of truth than that with which the large majority of the educated are imbued. This is being demonstrated in the existing political contest in California—in fact, all over the American Union. The illiterate many are struggling to overturn the plundercratic *regime*, as an indispensible prerequisite to any reforms; whilst most of the literate or educated (not, however, the best thinkers among them) are striving to perpetuate that *regime*, and thus estop or render nugatory all efforts at reform.

Denis Kearney and his Sand-lot surroundings are *sine qua non* appliances for achieving ulterior good results. Let these "ruffians" continue to yell, since such sounds the death knell of this plundercratic power.

Unable to disguise any sentiments I may entertain, I will here frankly admit that, looking, perhaps, some further and

clearer into futurity than the most of my fellow-citizens, and
impelled by a sacred animosity against the misrulers of the
country, whose power I seek to overthrow, I have of late come
to the conclusion that a more complete victory over the plundercrats and their chief agents—the lawyers, preachers, politicians and newspapers—can, ultimately, be obtained, should
these succeed, through their false and foul endeavors, in defeating the new Constitution. Such defeat will all the more
embitter, strengthen and consolidate the augmenting and upheaving Reform Party. Thousands who may be deceived into
voting against this Organic Act will, before September next,
have altered their opinions, and conclude to cast their ballots
for the new party candidates. We shall then sweep the State,
electing nearly every official. And provided men of sense and
nerve shall be sent to the Legislature, they will follow the example set by the plundercratic tools in that body and on the
Court benches, by ignoring the present Constitution, when
necessary, to rectify the huge wrongs these plundercrats have
committed, by reason of their setting aside or trampling upon
such instrument during the twenty-nine years of its existence.
Let them defeat the new Constitution at their peril !

And I will here enunciate some further prophetic specula-
tions.

Last June, just previous to the vote on the Convention call, I
advertised, in several newspapers, that I would deliver a discourse, outlining the plan of a Constitution which, if formed and
adopted, would end the angry class clashings in society, and
avert the impending internecine bloody revolution so threaten-
ingly approaching. I delivered that discourse in the 15th
District Court Room to a very small audience of which no
paper made mention. In it I predicted that should such order
of Constitution not be established (one in which independent
class suffrage, concurrent majorities and minority representation were the leading features), neither another sort of Constitution, if adopted, nor the present, should that be rejected,
would exist five years hence, and I now reiterate such prophecy.

A few days ago a member of Congress from Illinois proclaimed in the House of Representatives, that he believed the

present to be the last American Congress which would assemble. Perhaps it will, unless a government of widely different character shall early be established—one in which the explosive forces shall be removed—in which disrupting sectional and class antagonisms shall be provided against by clothing each with the absolute prerogative of defending itself. The grand old Roman Republic set us an example to follow, to be modified, of course, to suit our different civilization and other variant conditions.

This is the only system of government under which the poor, the producer and the honest can be properly protected.

Three alternatives lie before the American people to be speedily selected from.

1. A consolidated despotism, commencing, perhaps, with Grant at its head, who, if installed President, will, under the forms of a Republic, wield kingly or autocratic power. This is the style of government the bankers, merchants, large landholders, stock gamblers and the like, all favor.

2. To plunge into bloody anarchy, for an indefinite number of years, and bring unnumbered woes upon a fragmented Union and belligerant society, ending also with a Cæsar—or,

3. To establish the conservative and natural order of republican government, I have pointed out, and thus restore peace and prosperity to the distracted land.

This latter system of government I have, for a number of years, been advocating. The American people will I hope, early adopt it. *Ex necessitate Rei*—the necessity of the thing—will drive them to it. The existing fierce conflict of classes, in California, presage it. Normal institutions—legitimate and long lasting forms of government—spring from and grow up according to the genius and imperative needs of a people. An early fundamental alteration, in our civil polity, is inevitable, because the condition of affairs impel it. The rich and the poor, the high and the low, the strong and the weak, the intelligent and the ignorant will, alike, be protected under the system I have foreshadowed. When adopted, instead of filling our public stations with incompetent, unpatriotic, and immoral persons, each class will vie in selecting the purest and ablest representatives. This order of government will be self regulating, the natural antagonizing of the variant classes and interests compelling the adjustment of selfish differences on the equilibrium of justice to all.

Hence, that such natural, and, therefore, harmonizing system shall be the earlier adopted, it may be better that the submitted new Constitution shall be rejected, and, as elsewhere argued, that the Workingmen's Party shall secure a majority of the right sort of Representatives in the next Legislature, who will virtually set aside the existing Constitution and pay back the depredating rich, in their own coin, by passing discriminating laws against them, and thus compel them, as the Plebeians compelled the Patricians of Rome, to propose a compromise and inaugurate the plan of government suggested.

A perusal of that period in Roman history will exhibit an exact counterpart to the existing condition of affairs with us. Like our Shoddy Aristocracy, the Patricians seized upon the most of the unoccupied Public Lands, which, as with us, were held a common estate of all. They evaded the payment of their due share of taxes and compelled the oppressed Plebeians to pay most of the expenses of government. They made and executed all the laws in accordance with their selfish purposes. They used the police force and the army to suppress any murmurings of discontent on the part of the Plebeians—imputing to their menacing but just demands, the disorders of society and sufferings of which they complained. They fined, imprisoned, or banished such of their prominent leaders whom they could not or did not buy, and broke up orderly meetings convened to take measures to secure redress of grievances. The parallel may be further extended. In Rome, as with us, the most of the lawyers, politicians, priests and penmen were, at such period, the pensioned servitors of the malgoverning Patricians.

I have stated an oft quoted truism—that history repeats itself. We are about repeating, in America, one or the other of the two most important pages recorded in the annals of humanity. To the first I have alluded. It was that memorable epoch in ancient Rome, when the long oppressed Plebeians finding all other efforts to ameliorate their condition inefficacious, resolved to appeal to arms. The entire Roman state was on the eve of being plunged into a sanguinary conflict of classes when the Patricians agreed to cease their robberies and extortions, surrender much of the wrongfully monopolised Public Domain and share with the Plebeians an equal rule of the government, wherein the Patrician representatives continued, as hitherto, to make all the laws, but the absolute veto of such as were construed to not operate justly upon each class was vested in the representatives of the Plebeians. Thus was Rome then saved from the spilling of one drop of fraternal blood, and the foundation was laid for that imperial world-conquering Republic, which endured for centuries, and the genius of whose language, literature, religion, arts, arms, laws and civil polity, has largely dominated all Christendom, ever since.

The other grand event was the terrific French Revolution inaugurated in 1789 — the bounden effect of a long series of years of misrule and oppression by Kings, Ministers, Noblemen and wealthy Commoners ; who, to the last, refused to hearken to the groaning plaints and agonizing petitions for redress, resounding throughout the Kingdom during that lengthy period.

It is for our so-called Patricians or Nobility—the bar sinister blooded Plutocrats—to say which of these alternatives they intend to accept. Their present blinded Bourbonism looks as if the latter. And it is my strong conviction that it must, inevitably, come to this, why I, after several years of active and prominent efforts to get up the late Constitutional Convention, have not been more active, prompt and prominent in securing the popular indorsement of its labor. For I once again proclaim—let the plundercrats defeat it if they dare, it will be the worse for them.

But they will do it if they can, for demented by their inordinate avarice and shortsighted selfishness they seem oblivious to all the signs and portents of the times. We have recently had an exemplification East of this blinded and demented conduct of the large capitalists. The telegram stated that a combination of them had agreed to take many millions of the United States four per cent. Bonds as a safer investment thau any other securities, though the latter pay larger interest.

Now, if town, county, State and individual corporation securities are endangered, by reason of our social, political and financial disturbances, are not these Federal Bonds, likewise, in danger of depreciation or becoming entirely worthless? If the credit and stability of the others, which are the foundations on which the Federal superstructure is reared, be undermined or shall rot away, will not such superstructure fall ? In fact the sovereign States, the creators of the Federal Government, will survive, in some form, though such creature of them shall perish.

In Union Hall the other night our renegade Governor demagogically told the depositors in the Savings Banks that the adoption of the New Constitution would break up such institutions and compel them to invest in U. S. four per cents.

It has been the fashion of several of the plundercratic organs and other servitors of such dynasty, to denominate Kearney as a sort of California Jack Cade, because he has spoken so denunciatorily of law books, lawyers and other educated men. But ought he and his associates to be censured for this? Have they not witnessed that these law books, lawyers, judges, editors and most other writers and educated men are the staunch sustainers of our thieving Dollarcrat nobility and their vile misgovernment of the country ? Where do you find the great majority of such to-day, in California?—doing violence to their consciences by selling their abilities to uphold the existing rotten condition of affairs. These men and papers do not term me an "agrarian," "ignoramus," a "blatherskite" nor a "knave," and yet I indorse pretty much all of Kearney's Jack Cadean philippics against them.

They deserve the worst that he has said about them, and a great deal more. In fact, the greatest fault I have to find with Agitator Kearney, is, that he has not been sufficiently denunciatory of these "daylight robbers and midnight thieves." He, like myself, has some genius in coining words and phrases, with which to more properly depict the villains. Let him invent some new ones.

These arrant and unspeakable rascals threaten that, in the event of the adoption of the New Constitution, they will take their cash and flee the State. The fact is such, penitentiary and gallows-deserving knaves well know they have *got* to go in the event of the new order of men and affairs attaining to power in California, or take the consequences of remaining; and are thus paving the way with excuses for their intended sudden leave taking. But we don't intend these contemplating *emigres* shall take their stolen booty with them. They must disgorge such plunder before going.

It is a conceded fact that nearly all the capitalists of California are the meanest, most sordid, most avaricious and most dishonest on the surface of the globe. There may be some worse in hell; several of ours have gone there.

Kearney has, also, denounced the Clergy, and advantage has sought to be taken of this to prejudice Church members against him and his party. But do not the most of the priesthood, Catholic, Protestant and Hebrew, pander to and side with the plundercrats in opposing the New Constitution and the reform movement ? This was to be expected. They are the counterparts of that pharisaic set, against whom the great Nazarine Reformer thundered his anathemas throughout Judea, eighteen hundred and fifty years ago. " Wo! unto ye, scribes, phari. sees, hypocrites, lawyers, unjust judges, money changers, usuers and land monopolists," spake that immaculate man-like God or God-like man, whichever he may be titled. Where would he stand if in our midst to-day? As fiercely assailing these same classes here as he did then and there.

Some of these whited sepulcher Anti-Christs oppose the New Constitution, because enough of God is not recognized in it. Better these fellows get a little of God put in their hypocritcal hearts.

And some of these same unconscionable hypocrites have been making a simulated sacrilegeous outcry against the " Passion Play," recently acted in this city; and illegally using the municipal authority to prevent it.

Foremost among such pious pretenders, is Supervisor Rountree, Deacon in Doctor Scott's Church, and a Front Street merchant. Now, if this fellow will, instead of running a religious muck against the Passion Play, cease assisting the Water Works Company, Gas Works Company, and other roguish monopolists, to rob the people of San Francisco, which he has been doing since the day he was inducted into office, he will stand a better chance of getting to heaven, provided he ever did or can have such chance.

And how inconsistent are these same piety pretenders who object to the "Passion" personification, performed, in the main, by members of the Old Mother Church, and not objected to by its Clergy, yet attended, in that same theater, to listen to the travesty of the Bible, his ribald jestings and infidelic scoutings at all religious sentiment by Col. Robert Ingersoll.

Kearneyism, so-called, is an effect—a natural and bounden effect—and not a cause of the tumultuous and distressing times on which we have fallen. The causes I have enumerated in this discourse. These causes are the men and their vile system and doings herein set forth. And those who most deprecate Kearneyism are the most responsible for producing such bounden effects. The plundercrats who have ruled this State from its foundation, are its really criminal element—its most dangerous class of society. I have, for thirty years, been pointing this out, and asservating it in all my writings.

The utilization of Kearneyism is but a means to an end. It is an alterable medicine; a sort of drastic purge, to work off the unhealthy humors of the body politic.

This turbulent and purifying ordeal has long been foreseen and predicted by others as well as by myself. Again and again during the past near third of a century, have I sent forth pamphlet after pamphlet, and article after article, through newspaper medium, warning the misrulers of the country of what would, ere long, be the bitter fruits borne of their bad planting. But the only response to such monitions was to instruct their hireling newspaper and politicians to characterise me as being sour-tempered, disappointed, insane, a false prophet, bird of ill-omen and the like. They also titled me a misanthropean Ishmalite, an incendiary and would-be disturber of the peace.

These bitter fruits are now ripening and must be eaten by those who cultivated them. As they have sown so shall they reap.

Let these plundercrats and their minions continue to call for the police and the military to put down this revolution of their origination; they will call in vain, because the people—the long defrauded and misruled masses—are arising, in their might and anger, to overthrow such crying evil. *Vae Victis!*

True, these masses are themselves to blame for ignoring men of virtue and high intellect, and filling their public stations, as a rule, with knaves or fools; but, as history teaches, they will not permit such self-blame to operate as an estoppel to this movement, but will vent their vengeful anger against the demagogues and wealthy plunderers who have deceived, misruled and robbed them. And what effrontery for these very plunderers, their subsidized newspapers and official tools to now come forward and taunt the people for having voted to put themselves in office and thus keep up a system so much complained of.

We are entering a transitionary period, in which momentous social and political changes will occur. The Bourbon class will, of course, oppose these changes—will war against the hand of destiny—will strive to stifle such bounden birthings. But these impotent fools and knaves had as well strive to stay the inrolling tides of the ocean.

Old parties are crumbling to pieces. New combinations are being formed of affinitive elements. The Bourbons and plundercrats East, as well as in California, are consolidating their forces to maintain the *status in quo*, and have adopted the deceptive appellation of "Non-Partisans," yet, are partisans of the strictest order.

These old Bourbons have been sneeringly terming, for several years, the constantly increasing dissatisfied and justly complaining many, Adullamites. We accept such appellation. Our prototypes, in ancient Jewry, from whence this title is derived, had such excellent cause for their complainings—precisely the same as with us—as to, at length, achieve a victory, under the gallant David, over the embattled hosts of persecuting and oppressing Bourbon Saul. And so it will be here. The Adullamites will win.

I have.said that the two old parties, in California, are rotten to the core ; but candor compels me to admit that the once grand old Constitutional party to which I have so long belonged, and whose principles have faithfully defended—the Democratic—is the more debased and debauched, by reason of having the more recreant leaders. Both, for several years, have been manipulated according to the imperial ukases of Leland Stanford. A few years ago Stanford was threatened with a noosed rope by the old band of plundercrats of San Francisco, because he had said, in one of his railroad manifestos, that the city had been built upon the wrong side of the Bay ; and had signified the intention of securing Goat Island for a railroad terminus, and, consequently, building up a rival city there. But, after being bulldosed and bounced to abandon this design, and resolving to make his road terminus in San Francisco, removing his company's headquarters to it, and he and his prime ministers erecting their palaces in its midst, he was then chosen and crowned their grand imperial chieftain. Thus supported, this puissant potentate has long absolutely ruled the politics of the State. Through Gorham, Sargent, Page, Stowe, Gage, Abell, Boruck and others, including some forty or fifty newspapers—the *Record-Union* at the head—he runs the Republican party ; and through Gwin, Irwin, Farley, Lewis, McCoppin, Maynard, Curtis and others, including some score or more uewspapers—the San Francisco *Examiner* at their head—the Democratic.

Just nine years ago (30th March, 1870) I addressed a large assemblage—mostly mechanics and common laborers—from the tumbling walls of a cemetery vault, on the now world-heralded Sand Lot of San Francisco. It had been the city burial place, and was then called Yerba Buena Park. A synopsis of that speech was published in the next day's *Evening Bulletin*. In it I counselled them to organize independently in order to better make headway against thieving monopolists and their chief agents, the lawyers, politicians and newspaper proprietors. But the time was not then ripe for action, nor had they an efficient leader. Both are now at hand, and in the Book of Fate it is written this party shall succeed.

THE PLUNDERCRATS MUST GO!

A word in explanation of my crusading exclamation.

As the greater includes the lesser, as causes control effects, so I sum the leading shibboleth of the Workingmen's party—"The Chinese must go"—as well as the other great evils afflicting the land, in my Catonian cry—

THE PLUNDERCRATS MUST GO!

This is my *Delenda est Carthago* war note.

APPENDIX A.

[Extracts from a Pamphlet published Address to the Legislature.]

Assembly Concurrent Resolutions, No. 35.—Introduced by Mr. Tully, February 6th, 1874.—Relative to title in fee of the Government to Public Lands and Municipal and Intercommunication Monopolies.

Resolved, by the Assembly, the Senate concurring, That the public lands of the United States are not held in absolute fee by the Government, to be given or sold in unlimited quantities by the Congress thereof, but are in the nature of a joint or common estate possessed by the entire people, and can only be segregated and parceled out among such people, in limited quantities, under rules and regulations prescribed by said Congress, acting as a fiduciary agent; that the spirit of our laws, and the genius of our institutions, long since determined that one hundred and sixty acres is the maximum quantity allotted to an individual occupant, which occupant is alone entitled to receive the patent therefor ; and hence all public lands otherwise alienated have been in violation of this trust and agency, and should, where held in larger tracts than 160 acres, revert to the common estate to be thus parceled out and possessed.

Resolved, That the great highways of intercommunication, whether of persons, property, or intelligence—navigable lakes and rivers, canals, railways, turnpikes and telegraphs—should be free and open to all persons at a minimum rate of charge, and subject to no exclusive nor undue corporation or monopoly profits and tolls; and that the incorporated governments of towns and cities should own and conduct all street Railways, Waterworks, Gasworks, and other public municipal requirements.

Resolved, That the Governor is hereby requested to forward a copy of these Resolutions to each of our Senators and Representatives in Congress.

*   *   *   *   *

The Resolutions under consideration, relative to the primary tenure in the public domain; monopoly profits on lines of intercommunication, and the corporate ownership of municipal franchises, are an exact transcript of those presented last session by Mr. Days. I am their author. The ideas embodied therein have long been entertained by me, and often sought to be made public ; but no newspaper proprietor would permit their enunciation through his columns, until some five or six years ago, when I persuaded the owner of the *Golden City*—a San Francisco literary weekly—to let me insert them in his paper. The same were promulgated in a political pamphlet issued by me during the Gubernatorial canvass of 1871. And the leading papers of the State, including certain pseudo-reforming ones, are still in opposition to them. Having largely assisted in such plunderings of the public lands, these open and covert organs of the plunderers are, of course, inimical to any measure calculated to enforce a disgorgement of this booty—some of them, doubtless, holding a goodly share of the same. The Resolutions were indefinitely postponed last session, by a vote of thirty-four to thirty. I hope that no such evasion of an expression upon their merits will be permitted this session. The lawyers, including judges, will, of course, nearly all oppose them. I look for nothing different in connection with any genuine reform measure from this Bourbonic class. With all their reading and intelligence and profession of love of justice, where do you find them standing in those great upheavings of a people against the grinding oppressions of a long endured malgovernment ? Always, with rare individnal exceptions, upon the side of wrong, and staunchly maintaining the *status in quo* or letter of inequitable enactments and decreements. Consequently, whenever these up-rising oppressed communities obtained the mastery, their first avenging acts were to burn the law books and court records, and kill all the judges and lawyers they could lay their hands on ; except some cunning and dissembling few of the demagogic order, who suddenly mount the cresting wave of the onrolling revolution and enrank themselves among the foremost and most radical, because the prospect for pay, as well as safety, appears to be better upon that side. But these menacing popular commotions teach nothing, give no monitions to the body of the lawyers.

The great and good Judean reformer (carpenter Joseph's puta-tive son), when thundering his fierce anathemas and terrible invectives against that trio of oppressors and despoilers—the pharisaic priesthood, usurious money changers, and the lawyers—was not alone unheeded in his prophetic warnings, but crucified through their instigation, for seeking to disturb '' vested rights,'' and the *status in quo* of such men's upholding. Nemesis, however, soon overtook this triumvirate of wrong-doers, as well as the de-bauched and blinded multitude who followed their lead ; just as she threatens to soon pour out her vials of wrath upon this same triumvirate and their dupes in our land, at this day.

In wholesome eras, when laws are properly made and admin-istered, the conserving proclivities of lawyers render them the best class in a community. But when, in degenerate eras, such as ours is in this land, where an intellectual and moral taint enpermeates the whole of society ; where the governmental system is abnormal, and law is perverted in its making and administering; when the dispen-sation of injustice instead of justice becomes the rule of the courts, then this conserving sentiment and action render them the worst class. Their education teaches them to maintain every abuse prac-ticed under the *forms* of law. Court decrees, however wrong, must, in their opinion, be held inviolate, unless regularly set aside by other court decrees. And even not then, should so-called '' vested rights'' have intervened, when they raise those canting, swindling and estopping outcries of '' *stare decisis !*'' '' *res adjudi-cata !*'' '' *ex post facto* laws !'' and '' vested rights !'' and thus essay to perpetuate wrong and encourage wrong-doing. Having dishonestly acquired this property through the forms of prostituted law, they and their clientelles hypocritically profess their " sacred regard" for the " rights" thuswise obtained.

The big gun lawyer and Boanerges orator of the Assembly, (Norton), a " Dolly Varden" reformer too, informed me that he would oppose the first resolution, because it was revolutionary in character and disturbed " vested rights." I responded that it *was* of revolutionary tendency, but denied that it disturbed any vested *rights*, but would annul the vested wrongs, frauds, robberies and rascalities through which this vast domain had, by lawyer instrumentality and false legal appliances, been transferred to speculators. For over a score of years, as well and widely known, I constantly combatted this thievery. But of what avail? So far from stopping it, each year witnessed some new device for plundering these acres, and that in still huger quantities. Hence, long since ceased such fruitless effort. And why longer continue this now delusive outcry about putting a stop to such farther fraudulent alienation of this common heritage of the whole people, since almost all the remaining arable area of such vast domain has already been passed into the hands of legalized spoliators ? It is like making a fuss about locking the stable door after the horse has been stolen. And of what use the further investigation of the many fraudulent and otherwise illegal transactions connected with this transferance ? Everybody knows them to be true, and likewise knows or ought to know that but little good land remains to this *cestui que* estate, by reason of such faithless action of the trustees of it.

*   *   *   *   *

The relevancy of my assailment of the lawyers and certain other classes in connection with this subject, will be perceived by every one of the least intelligence. These are the persons who have exploited and appropriated this vast domain, and who will oppose its restitution.

We have no titled and exclusively privileged patrician class in America, but are despotically and injuriously ruled by an infinitely worse one than was ancient Rome, in her most degenerate days—an oligarchy of mere wealthy men—individual and corporate. And these exploiting and all-grasping capitalists are chiefly composed of the meanest blooded and and most unprincipled portion of the population. But mark their mighty power. For years, municipal, State and Federal Governments have been absolutely under their control. Their primary agents in acquiring and abusing this power have been the lawyers, newspaper editors and the priesthood ; the secondary and completing ones, our recreant law makers and administerers, which latter include many of the former. From President and Chief Justice* of the Union down to the pettiest magistrate and constable, all, more or less, bow to this plutocratic dominancy. Congress and the Legislatures yield to this potent influence. This Legislature, if not possessing as much talent as some former ones, doubtless contains as much honesty, in the aggre-

---

* The present Chief Justice, Waite, is proving an excepitno.

gate ; yet, notwithstanding a large portion of it was expressly
elected to reform the many abuses practiced by California's moneyed
masters, there is not, I greatly fear, moral courage enough in it to
dare properly assail these infamous tyrants and their official servitors. Too little of the heroic and self-sacrificing spirit of a Grac-
chi animates any of you. True, you are running a sort of blind,
vindictive muck against railroad proprietary extortions and dicta-
tions; but, as hereafter observed, I look for no good results in this
to follow soon, nor in the way you seek, for the reason that you are
warring against effects instead of causes, and lesser effects at that.

There is no justice in the land! What moneyless and, therefore, uninfluential person, dare take a rich one into our courts to
assert a right to property of large value, with any strong hope or
certainty of obtaining a decision in his or her favor, though
all the law, the evidence and the equity shall be upon that side ?
Whence has arisen that stereotyped expression constantly made
in California to such impoverished suitors—"*It matters not how
much right may be upon your side, you are bound to lose your suit,
because there is too much money against you.*"

(I will here add, *en parenthesis*, that since penning this declara-
tion, the Supreme Court of California has verified it in the case of
the victim now adressing you. With long deferred and heart sick-
ening hope, he thought that such case might prove an exception to
this latter day judicial rule. And I may, likewise, significantly ad-
dend, that three of my opponents in it are—first, General D. D.
Colton, a one-millionaire, and also the political right bower of
Stanford & Co., in their railway management ; second, Judge S. C.
Hastings. a five-millionaire, who, when on the Supreme Bench
himself, was reputed to have the doorway to his judicial chamber,
and his conscience, constantly unlocked by the "Golden Key" of
successful suitors ; and who has the reputation of opening more
similar entrances to his successors, with the same instrument, than
any man in California; and, thirdly, Michael Reese, a ten-million-
aire. Additional, also, stands the Hibernia Bank, with its fifteen
millions deposit power, and twenty millions aggregate fortunes of its
directory and stockholders. So you'll perceive there was, indeed,
" too much money" against me. Providence and victory, remarked
Napoleon, are usually upon the side of the heaviest battallions. Victory, in our California high courts, appears to generally side with
the heaviest money bags. A false decision has never been rendered in California, prolific as this State has been in such unright-
eous rulings. The plainest constructions of law and equity are
thrust aside therein. It will be reversed. Injustice and corruption
cannot always rampantly rule among us. " It is a long lane which
has no turning." But we need not look for any such turning, so
long as our judicial seats shall alone be filled from the ranks of professional, practicing and champerty-entangled attorneys, unless the
monitory and minatory terrorum examples of other peoples shall be
adopted, in order to hang the sword of Damocles over the heads of

our judges. If this be done, I would especially recommend the plan pursued by King Cambyses of Persia, who had a corrupt Chief Justice skinned alive, and the skin fastened over the judgment seat, for his successors to sit upon, and thus be always warningly reminded of his fate, and what caused it.) [See Appendix E.]

Here is where reform is imperiously and most demanded. For what are nearly all our high Courts but intrenched strongholds—protecting citadels of America's freebooting Moneycrats, who, when hard pressed, always flee to and find safe shielding beneath the smirched robes of the treacherous officials placed there by the people ; and from whence these robbers, armed with weapons and ammunition obtained from them, constantly sally forth in new forays upon the community. They are infinitely worse marauders than those European robber Barons in the middle ages ; since one might successfully resist the levying of the latter, whereas, by reason of these cunning latter-day depredators leaguing with so many of our law-makers and dispensers, the property of the masses is placed completely at the mercy of such legalized freebooters.

* * * * *

But go on with your circumscribed and halting efforts at reform. BEWARE ! There is a higher and more summarily acting body to supervise and do the work which you law makers and the five judicial interpreters of it, sitting in a chamber beneath, shall prove derelict in performing—the grand Comitia or Forum Populi, the People, in revolutionary parliament assembled. And since history repeats itself, the lessons of the past all give warning that this *dernier resort* is rapidly approaching in our land. If you, Messieurs Representatives, would prevent or stave it off, then dare and do your duty. But I fear you will not. Already three-fourths of the session has passed, and what of much merit has been performed ? What real rectification of the scourging afflictions of misgovernment, under which the people groan, has been attempted ? If between now and the adjournment you do not go forward more boldly and wisely, you will find yourselves kicking the beam when weighed in the public balance of deserts by your constituency. Do not deceive yourselves with the conception that retrenching the expenditures of the Government—truly, a much needed reform—is the paramount object desired. As usual, too, a mass of time consuming, thought-engrossing and expensive local and other special legislation, is being enacted this session, and I suspect that many members make the mistake in supposing that quantity, instead of quality, will satisfy the people. You must rise to a higher plane of observation, have more expanded views and resolve upon a bolder action, if you would achieve lasting fame for yourselves and benefit for your country.

One page more upon this point. Bacon, in his essay upon "Kingdoms and Estates,'' whilst arguing in favor of a titled, estated and exclusive privileged Nobility, who should be held strictly accountable for their high trust, observes that it would be to the State's disadvantage to have this Order too largely increased. Now, since the Lawyers compose the major portion of our untitled nobility—have become too numerous, and, like the degenerate and selfish Patricians in certain periods of Roman history, have allied themselves with the more powerful vulgar wealthy—the " Shoddy Aristocracy " of America—in order to unfairly seize, through the forms of unconstitutional laws, upon an undue share of this common landed property, as well as other assets of the country—especially, thereby, despoiling the great producing or industrial classes, the creators of all wealth—it is time for these defrauded masses to arise in their might and anger and subvert such predacious dynasty, even if to effect it they shall be driven to the extreme measures forced upon the French people near the latter portion of the last century.

B.
HONORS DIVIDED.

The *Chronicle*, in its leading editorial the 11th of May, contains the following : " It should be remembered by all that the late election is emphatically the verdict of the producing classes of this State. The farmers are entitled to the first place in the roll of honor."

I am the son of a farmer, a farmer once myself, and, as my writings all attest, and as thousands of farmers and other producers personally well know, have ever been the ardent advocate of the producing classes, especially in sympathy with the agricultural ; consequently, am better qualified than the *Chronicle* to pass an opinion in the premises.

The extract is only partially correct. Such verdict *was* the achievement, chiefly, of the producing classes ; but it sorrows me to say that the farmers are *not* entitled to the " first place in the roll of honor " for initially organizing to secure the important victory won. During several years I vainly strove to have them thus independently organize, and invite co-operation of the labor element and others of the cities. Additional to appeals to them through print, I often went among them to urge this action. I attended several State Granger Sessions to counsel, as an outsider, with their leading men to prompt them to it, but was met with the response that, their Order being non-political, they could not move in the matter. I asked them what good such Order could accomplish unless it became a political power. They, at length, began to perceive that no good would or could be accomplished unless it did discuss and advocate measures of governmental reform—their late State Lecturer, Wright, and present Lecturer, Pilkington—both sensible and excellent citizens—strongly indorsing such procedure. Moreover, as I, from their first organization in the States, found out and said often to the honest " Brothers," the Grange influence was insidiously used by the traitors among them to subserve the political schemes of their enemies.

In the last Legislature were near forty Grangers, about four-fifth of Democratic persuasion, the others of the Republican. I wrote, as did Wright in concert with me, letters to numbers of these, arguing with and imploring them not to go into caucus to nominate a

U. S. Senator, as a corrupt servitor of the Railway Companies and other corporations would assuredly thereby be chosen ; but to keep out, and by holding the balance of power dictate a different result. Wright and I, on the eve of such caucuses being held, went to Sacramento to use the same argument in person ; but the old party ties proving stronger than their Granger faith, and other influences, which should have counselled a different action, the entire contingent went into the two traps set for them—the one choosing, out of "compliment," a candidate inimical to the productive interests, and the other nominating and electing an old intriguing professional politician, notoriously known as a devoted servitor of the Central Pacific Railway Company.

And what solitary good thing did those, near one hundred, rural representatives in that Legislature accomplish ? I know of not one. They helped to do much that was bad. Additional to electing Farley Senator, they, largely, voted for the infamous "Gag Law," designed to stifle the nucleus or incipient rallying of that grand army which has just achieved the splendid victory the *Chronicle* so justly boasts of, but would rob the initial organizers of it, of the honor due to them. The *Chronicle* itself advocated the passage of that impotent enactment of the affrighted plundercrats, and howled as lustily as any of their organs for the seizure, trial and sending to the penitentiary, under its provisions, of Denis Kearney and comrades. In fact, this paper boasted that it had inspired the origination in this city, by the plundercrats, of the two projected Acts taken by District Attorney Murphy and a delegation of Supervisors to Sacramento, to be rushed through the Legislature in hot haste. The draft of the one prepared by Murphy and the *Chronicle* proprietors, which became a law, was much worse than that enacted, the Assembly having modified it ; whilst the other, which made it a misdemeanor—subjecting a person to fine or imprisonment for speaking disrespectfully of a judge in a company of more than five persons—was too strong a dose for even the servile Senate to swallow.

These faithless farmer representatives—that is, the most of them —not content with such recreant conduct in the halls of legislation, came outside 10 sneer at the Workingmen's meetings held on Sunday in front of the Capitol, where I several times spoke, but vainly endeavored to induce some of those Grangers join with me in starting the movement towards obtaining the great victory in the "late verdict of the producing classes of this State."

I have mentioned in the Introduction, and heretofore in this Appendix, the divertment of the Granger organization from any useful purpose, in consequence of so many of its leading members being in the pay and service of the C. P. R. R. Co.—that company buying them up by freighting their wheat, wool, fruit, wine, etc., and themselves, at half rates, or no rates, and charging extra heavy rates to others to make up the deficiency. In the same way this company bought up Wm. T. Coleman & Co., and a few other influential merchants, to assist in upholding their extortioning power, and then made up such losses from the pockets of the other merchant freighters.

This, and because large numbers of farmers did not belong to the Grange organization, prevented any concerted action being taken among them to make headway against the long-complained of robberies and pollutions of the plundercrats, until the Workingmen of San Francisco inaugurated the revolt against their further misrule.

It is true that superior credit should be given the farming element for earlier favoring the call for a Constitutional Convention. Ten years ago I commenced laboring to secure this result, mainly as a revolutionary starter, and whilst suceeeding, with a few other agitators of the question, in largely arousing the rural population to take such action, the urban was either opposing or quiescent and indifferent. Four years ago the people (mostly a farmer vote) did *constitutionally* demand the assembling of such Convention : but a corrupt and assinine Legislature, influenced by the C. P. R. R. and other big corporations, the Supreme Court Judges and other corporation attorneys, as well as most of the newspapers (*Chronicle* included), induced it to declare otherwise—contending that a majority of all the votes cast were requisite, instead of a majority voting on the proposition. The question was resubmitted (it never would have been permitted had the plundercrats for a moment imagined it would have carried), when, chiefly, through the vote and influence of the farmers (strongly, again, opposed by the *Chronicle*), it received such latter majority. But still the farming element, blindly wedded to the two rotten old parties, would have achieved nothing of material benefit, except for the bold new departure taken by the Workingmen of San Francisco, under the aggressive leadership of Denis Kearney, of severing all connection with those parties and organizing a new one.

Thus the honors are divided between these two great productive or manual labor classes of the community ; and their interests being identical, there should be no antagonisms between them, only a generous rivalry as to which shall choose the ablest, purest and bravest men to represent them.

The very issue I labored for years to bring to a head was joined during the late short and sharp campaign, and is being refought the present. I have stronger faith in the Workingmen's party battling such opposition *a l'outrance*, than will the *Chronicle* and its coadjutors—the leaders and rank and file of a to-be-organized "Constitution Party." In truth, I have no shadow of faith in the sincerity of the *Chronicle's* course. *It intends treachery to the interests it now pretends to subserve.* I fully believed so all during the late campaign, and so declared to many.

Let the antecedents of this, the foulest journal ever published in California, indicate its genuine animus.

C.

RAILROAD COMMISSION.

Having so many years taken a prominent part in Railway matters —publishing a vast amount of matter thereon, and attended, as a Lobbyist, several Legislatures to counsel proper action in relation to them; and having been the *first* and *only* person, during several years, to advise the creation of such a Commission as has been provided for in the new Constitution, I feel authorized to speak some further regarding this deeply important question, now that the time approaches for the State to assume its legitimate control over such corporations.

And first, a short summary of history to prove the proud distinction I claim as the prime inspirer of the creation of this Commission. On the last page of the Pamphlet published, "*Address to* the Legislature," laid before that body the 1st March, 1874, is to be found the following:

"In conclusion, I will abbreviately and also diffidently, because feeling myself unequal to the task of solving so great a problem, treat upon that portion of the second resolution which relates to telegraphs and railroads. The former, in my opinion, should, as in England, belong, absolutely, to the Government and become a portion of the postal service. And why not so, to a certain extent, the latter, those, at least, which the Government, State or Federal, has helped to build? At any rate the Government should have a representation in their Directory and actual management, in the ratio of its investment, and appoint superintending Commissioners to watch over those in which, it has none, in order to determine the *minimum* rates at which such roads can be operated. To give the absolute ownership and conduction of them to private parties and then undertake to regulate their freights and fares [by the Legislature] has always appeared to me to be absurd. The experiment, in this line, being attempted by the present Legislature, will prove abortive so far as achieving any of the results directly aimed at; but indirectly and remotely, good, I hope and believe, will flow from it."

That was the Session in which the famous "Freeman Bill," regulating fares and freights was so fiercely battled over, in as well as out the Legislative halls. The Railroad Companies expended vast sums in subsidizing Newspapers, Judges, Lawyers, Legislators and Lobbyists, to oppose such Bill, whose plea was that no power existed in the State to so control them. I opposed such latter assumption, but, whilst claiming the right of the Legislature to thus act, contended that it was impracticable of execution, directly, by that body. Nevertheless, I favored the passage of the Freeman Bill (for the reasons stated) after finding that not only not a solitary member in the Legislature but no one in all California or any of the other States, so far as I knew, sustained my views about such a Commission. The Bill passed the Assembly but was defeated in the Senate.

At the ensuing Session the same fierce and *costly* (to the R. Co.) controversy was had over the "Archer Bill." I was on hand again and took the same position as before. This, like the Freeman Bill, passed the Assembly but was defeated in the Senate.

By this time it began to dawn upon the minds of some that it was impracticable, though empowered with the prerogative, for the Legislature to regulate fares and freights, and some members commenced to advocate the creation of a Commission to do it. But the Railroad Janissaries in the Legislature, under the Captaincy of Farley—Stanford & Co.'s right bower in that body—and the well known veto to be looked for from his left bower in the capital—Governor Irwin—would not permit such a Commission to be projected ; consequently a sham, impotent and expensive Commission was, as a "tub to the whale" created, which authorized the Commissioners to find out and report that which every person in California already knew—that the Railroad operators were charging exorbitant and wrongly discriminating rates, as well as guilty of a great many other illegal and much hurtful practices.

I may add here, parenthetically, that such—"how not to do it" —sort of legislation, has, all along, been the rule in California, as well in City and County as State management. Notably has this been the action in regard to the water supply to the city of San Francisco. , To secure such State and City legislation and other serviceable rascality, the Spring Valley Water Company has expended at least two millions of dollars of bribery money during the past twenty-five years. As, elsewhere stated, the Railroad Company has expended about three million dollars of the same sort of money —all extorted from the people's pockets. And yet none of these rascals—bribers nor bribees—have been hung, nor even penitentiaried.

Subsequently to the adjournment of that 1876 Legislature, the important so-called "Granger Decisions," were rendered by the Supreme Court of the United States, which declared that each State possessed the sovereign right to regulate freights and fares within its boundaries, and to otherwise control as well as fix charges, for all public transportation agencies, even to Grain Elevators. These decisions were, of course, dissented from by that ever faithful, because regularly and heavily fed, corporation *Attorney-Judge*, Stephen J. Field.

Hence, of all the good work done by the Constitutional Convention, the creation of this Railroad Commission stands pre-eminent.

The next important action is for the people to select the right sort of Commissioners. It is a position of vast responsibility, more so than that of Governor. It even transcends, in importance, should it succeed in fully controlling these corporations, all the State offices combined, including the Courts and our Representatives in Congress, since the Railroad Companies having dominated or successfully defied all these, the people have delegated to such Commissioners the authority to dominate those Companies.

But such authority, provided that the ablest and faithfulest Commissioners shall be selected, can and will be negatived by the next Legislature, should not the popular vote send to such body a majority who will enact such a law as will enable the Commissioners to fulfil their duties.

The determination to entirely ignore certain sections and misconstrue the plainest provisions of others, has been openly proclaimed since adoption of the New Constitution, by various leading plundercratic papers. To this end they will move earth and hell to capture the Governorship, Legislature, Judiciary and Railroad Commission.

"We must capture the judiciary, gentlemen, capture the judiciary!" emphatically exclaimed "Duke" Gwin, in the recent secret "consultation of leading Democrats" held at the Cosmopolitan hotel. Meaning. thereby, venal tools for the Railway Company and other plundercrats.

The great powers lodged in the Chief Justice and the Railroad Commissioners are pronouncedly the Anti-New Constitutionists to be dangerous and unrepublican. I claim them to be eminently safe, conservative and republican. Elect the right sort of men to these positions and the weighty responsibility devolving upon them will all the more impel them to do their duty. This is in accordance with the natural law of our being as fully attested by many historical examples.

When the Plebeians of Rome had extorted from the Patricians an equal share in the government, the former elected two Tribunes who were clothed with the prerogative to examine all the laws framed by the Patricians and sanction only such as were deemed by them to be just ; their veto rejecting the others. These Tribunes long faithfully fulfilled this responsible function. In truth, it is questionable whether the Roman people rendered their liberties more secure or had better laws by subsequently increasing the Tribunate to three and again to ten. Twice when the Roman Republic was torn by intestine factions and, at the same time, imperiled by outside enemies, was Cincinnatus called to take, solely, the helm of affairs, and wisely and well did he steer the ship of State from off its endangering leeshore and breakers position. And these temporary Dictators were frequently so chosen, nearly all whom faithfully and well performed their great trust.

The State of Pennsylvania, which has suffered so much disgrace and injury by reason of the corruption of its Legislatures, sought to correct this by increasing the number of its members ; but recent developments demonstrate that the present numerous body is as corrupt and has passed as improper laws as any of its predecessors.

D.

NEWSPAPER POWER AND PERFIDY.

The time has passed for any newspaper in California, of the existing regime, to longer wield power. If the corrupt old politicians are to be thrown overboard, ought not these corrupt papers also ?

The public are awakening to a realizing sense of the infamy of both. These papers are too much permeated with every species of falshood; have been guilty of upholding too much rascality for one of them to be trusted as an exponent, adviser or leader in a reformatory movement. Moreover, all of them, in this city, *including the Agricultural Journals*, are supporters of the *bourgeoisie* or non-producing class, and, hence, are not to be trusted as supporters of the producing. How can the farmers of the State longer subscribe to such agricultural journals, after antagonizing themselves to the producing element, as they did during the recent Constitutional canvass?

How, then, can any citizen in California, who is earnestly seeking a radical change in affairs, place confidence in, much less submit to the lead and advisings of such a journal as the *Chronicle;* the most infamous sheet ever published west of the Rocky Mountains, or east, either.

It is an erroneous idea that its advocacy of the New Constitution secured a victory for such side, or added a vote to the majority given. That victory was decreed in the book of fate, and would have been achieved, had every newspaper in the State been on the other side.

The *Chronicle* happened to get on the victorious side, because, for some time previously, it had been at war with the plundercrats for refusing to longer pay its exorbitant blackmail or subsidy demandings, and because scenting success on the affirmative of the constitutional issue.

If the newspapers had carried any weight in the recent campaign, then ought the Constitution to have been overwhelmingly defeated, since there were ten times more of them circulated on such side than the opposite. And how came the Workingmen's Party to receive a majority vote in this city last June and elect twenty delegates outside of it, with all the papers in the State strongly opposing it ?

The only good the *Chronicle's* advocacy of the instrument did, was to arouse a fiercer conflict, and induce the various classes of society and the leading men of the State, to come out and exhibit their true colors. For this reason, I am glad the paper made such an able and aggressive fight upon our side; but I have no thanks to return it, because it was prompted to, and animated in such contest, by no spark of patriotism nor honesty of purpose.

It vexes and grieves me deeply to see so many talented and honorable citizens committing political suicide, at least, greatly damaging their reputation, by suffering themselves to be wheedled, humbugged and used, for their purposes, by the disreputable proprietors of that infamous journal.

E.

THE SWORD OF DAMOCLES—A CRETAN CUSTOM.

The figurative sword of Damocles should always be suspended over the heads of those in office; the good will not object nor fear its falling, whilst the bad will be deterred from doing wrong. But a literal sword must, occasionally, be made to descend and chop off some guilty heads, else 'twill lose its terrorum efficacy. Had the American people adopted that portion of the unwritten constitution or custom of ancient Crete, where once in twenty years the laws were suspended for the space of three days, when every strongly suspected malfeasant official or ex-official, who could not be proved guilty through regular processes of the law, was banished, hung or deprived of office, we should have had greater fidelity in our public servants, and preserved more purity among the people, as did such conserving custom in Crete.

Why not now inaugurate, at the beginning of this *bouleversement* era, such custom in California ? For example, let those generally believed (except by the *Chronicle* and its attorney, Aleck Campbell) guilty judges of the Supreme Court, be flayed, and their skins fas-

tened over five of the new judicial seats. The sixth should be covered with the flayed hide of that notoriously corrupt Ex-Chief
Justice S. C. Hastings, and ever since leaving the Bench its leading
" Broker." There are so many to choose from, deserving to cover
the seventh, that I leave the public to name the fitest. That arch-*judicial jesuit*, the corruptest judge among them all, and who has done
such infinite injury to California, and ruined such numbers by his
villainously false decisions, U. S. Supreme Court Justice Stephen J.
Field, might be named; but that the Persian Monarch's warning
plan may be adopted soon by the whole American people, for benefit
of their *Federal* judiciary, when the cuticle from the foul carcass of
Field will be wanted for use in the Washington Capitol.

F.

PLUTUISM vs. NIHILISM.

Our plundering plutocrats and their pensioned parvenus and
puppets are proving their sympathy with all forms of oppression by
denouncing the efforts of the Russian people to free themselves from
the horrid tyranny exercised by the government in that country.
The bloody ukases of their Emperor, and ruthless execution of them
by his military satraps, against which many in all ranks of society,
including some Noblemen, are revolting—are sanctioned by these
Plutus-plundercrats of ours, when sneeringly denouncing the
new Constitution supporters as Nihilists—the term by which the
liberty-struggling Russians are denominated. In truth, the dynasty
of these base-blooded *nouveau riche*, in America, is more despicable
than that of Russia or any country on the globe ; and they are
everywhere demanding, like the Czar of Russia, that the strong
arm of *force* shall be applied to repress the people's effort at reform.

G.

THE NEW NON-PARTISAN DODGE.

For ten years California has been under a sort of duumvirate
rule—that of Leland Stanford and Wm. M. Gwin. The two old
political parties in the State, during such period, have been manipulated as catspaws to subserve their purpose, and that of their co-
operating and sustaining plundercrats.

Their recently arranged scheme for duping the public again and
defeating any New Party, is to rally all of their liege retainers
around a so-called " Republican" ticket To this end the assembling of the Democratic State Convention, has, at the instance of the
Duumvirs, been postponed to the 1st of July, when a sham ticket *may*
be put forth, but the vote of all the obedient asses and knaves of
such rump party will be privately instructed to sustain the Republican nominees.

I hope my prediction as to this programme will prove correct as
it will finally squelch the bastard Democratic party in California.
But whether any shall cast a vote for a candidate put forth under

the name and guise of Republican or Democratic I wish once more
to say that such candidate cannot be otherwise than a supporter of
the old plundercratic regime.   None other can receive a nomination
from the Conventions of those parties.

H.
STATE RIGHTS.

There are two pledges that voters in September should exact
from candidates for the Legislature ; notwithstanding I am opposed
to the custom of pledging candidates for any office.

1st.   That under the Constitutional clause taxing Bonds, those of
the United States Government shall be included.   If Congress had
the right to exempt these Bonds from Federal taxation—which I
deny—it had no authority to say a State shall not tax those held by
its citizens or residents.   The Legislature should so declare.

2d.   The Legislature should also declare the sovereign right of
a State to prohibit the introduction into it of any people deemed by
it prejudicial to its welfare, and pass a law to prevent the coming into
it of the same.

I.
EMPTY BELLY ENLIGHTENMENT.

The mercenary penman of the plundercrats adduce all sorts of
sophistical and ingenious arguments and lying charges to prove
their opponents in the wrong.   But against their bald assertions,
personal denunciations, fine-spun theories and fanciful economic
problems, which they work out so satisfactorily to themselves, on
paper, I set the mother wit, instinctive convictions and empty
bellies of the masses.   Let these writers and talkers keep on trying
to prove that a stone is a piece of bread.   " The proof of the pud-
ding is in eating it."

J.
NON-RESIDENT REPRESENTATION.

As the new Constitution relegates to the respective counties all
their local legislation there is no longer reason why voters, in any
county shall not, if preferring, elect a non-resident to represent them
in the Legislature.   This system works well in Europe, securing a
higher order of talent and often faithfuller exponents of the views of
the majority in the voting district.   Let us adopt such system in
California.   If the suffragans in Siskiyou desire to send a representative to the Legislature whose residence is in Sacramento, San
Francisco, or Los Angeles, let them elect such.   Also, if desiring,
elect any of their county officers in the same way, after ascertaining
whether such persons will remove to their county and officiate if
elected.

'   It may be that some of the counties which gave large majorities
for the new Constitution will be compelled to vote for some non-
residents for their Superior Judges, else choose resident Attorneys

who antagonized such majority by opposing that instrument and otherwise proved themselves upholders of the old plundercratic dynasty. I suggested this new feature of election some years ago, but nobody would hearken to it then.

K.

SUICIDING OFFICIALS.

The guilty San Francisco officials are suiciding so rapidly (appalled and crazed at the detection and the fear of detection of their criminal practices) that none such may be left to receive their just deserts at the hand of the law when the day of reckoning shall have arrived.

It was less the exposures being made regarding the villainy of the Dupont street widening that dethroned the reason of Commissioner Maynard and impelled him to self-destruction than dread of the revelations to be made, erewhile, of the immeasurably greater juggling villainy perpetrated by the Water Supply Commission. Bryant and Murphy, of that Commission, will not go crazy nor suicide, because having no conscience left to be compuncted nor care for self or family disgrace.

These two worthies will await to learn whether the September election shall decree the instalment in office of a class of men who will do their duty in exposing and punishing the many and huge crimes committed by existing and ex-officials, when they will, along with scores of others, flee from the wrath to come. And come it will soon should such order of public servants then be selected. Nemesian compensation awaits these rascals.

California's thirty years saturnalia of official misrule and corruption is about to end—*Laus Deo!*

L.

THE VENAL *EXAMINER'S* LATEST EFFORT TO DISHONESTLY SERVE ITS MASTERS.

The Los Angeles *Herald*—one of Stanford & Co's subsidized organs, having, as a forlorn hope, suggested that the New Constitution might be construed so as to keep in place the twenty hold-over senators (fifteen or more of them being in the pay and service of the C. P. R. R. Company, the Spring Valley Water Company and other swindling corporations) the *Examiner* eagerly grasped at this straw and, with palpable insincerity stamped in its editorial, essayed to raise a doubt as to the clear reading of the letter of the Constitution and well-known intention of the members of the Convention, to get such construction placed upon the Section as would retain those corrupt senators.

M.

MEN OF SUBSTANCE.

The *Chronicle* calls upon its embryotic party, for which it acts as

midwife and dry nurse, to send only men of "substance" as delegates to their State Convention. Here is the plundercratic idea indorsed of having none but men of property—the richer the higher
ranked—to run the government ; and they commence, at once, to
practice upon this idea by choosing Marion Biggs, the great Butte
county land monopolist, as Chairman of their State Executive Com-
mittee, and John H. Burke its Secretary. Burke is one of the
Chronicle editors and a man of vast *prospective* " substance," having a $34,000,000 suit in Court against the bonanza Barons.
The fact is, that whilst many of the best citizens in the interior of
the State are joining the " New Constitution Party," it will, under
the incubation of the buzzard-hawk *Chronicle*, hatch out nothing
good. The signs, at present, are indicating that numbers of the
old straightout Democrats, who voted against the Constitution, are
about making overtures to connubiate with the *Chronicle's* bastard
bantling. Let the farmers and others interior repudiate the *Chronicle*, and then a harmonious co-operation can be had with the Workingmen's organization.

N.

FALLING BETWEEN THREE STOOLS.

The *Chronicle*, like others, " whose vaulting ambition o'erleaps
itself," essayed to stand on three stools at the same time. Mounting
the Workingmen's party, for a start, it next managed to draw along-
side the great agricultural element as a second tool. Straddling
these, it then bulldosed the hostile *bourgeoisie* of San Francisco
into being a third stool for this striding Colossus to sceptre from.
But just when imagining its tripod throne secure, the stools separate,
and down will tumble this too ambitious aspirant.

O.

CAMPBELL'S PUFFERY OF THE JUDGES.

It is noticeable that the *Chronicle*, during the recent campaign, had
nothing to say against our notoriously corrupt Supreme Court
Judges. It has suggested Judge Rhodes as a candidate on the Republican ticket for Governor, and, doubtless, would like to see
several of the others again placed on the Bench they have so much
befouled. The night the *Chronicle's* standing attorney, Aleck
Campbell, delivered his speech in Platt's Hall, he loftily eulogized
three of them—Wallace, McKinstry and Crockett—as honorable,
high-toned and intelligent jurists ; but who vouches for Campbell.

P.

SACKING THE ENEMY'S CAMP.

The action of the piebald "New Constitution Party" leaders, in
proprosing to make one more combined assault upon the plundercratic
forces merely to disperse them, secure the offices, and then break
ranks, is like a freebooting army of allied mercenaries, which, hav-

ing routed the enemy, stop short in their career of victory to pillage the captured camp, divide the spoils and then disband.

A THIRD PRESIDENTIAL PARTY.

The signs indicate that a third Presidential ticket will be nominated next year, founded chiefly on the leading issue joined in this State—the producing against the non-producing classes. In such event will not an appropriate name for the new party be—THE PRODUCTIVE. And who superior to GEORGE W. JULIAN, of Indiana, for its nominee ? I am in favor of the formation of such party, Julian being my first choice for its Presidential candidate; and Wade Hampton, of South Carolina, its Vice-Presidential.

Q.

BENNETT, HOWARD AND TERRY.

In my discourse I highly eulogized these eminent citizens, and suggested them as the worthiest to occupy seats on the Supreme Court bench. At that time this opinion was applauded by all the supporters of the new Constitution. The character of those men has undergone no change since. They are still the same able lawyers, polished scholars and honorable gentlemen. Why, then, should not every voter opposed to the existing villainous order of affairs in California cast a ballot for them, whether nominated by the Workingmen's party or the "New Constitution" party ? I intend to do so, and thousands, like myself, are determined to cut loose from the trammels of all parties and party conventions and vote their first preferences This is the only way to compel the nomination of proper candidates. Should the Workingmen's Conventions—State and county—place exceptionable nominees on their tickets, as the result of secret clique scheming or one-man dictation, let them be at once repudiated, and let a few earnest and sensible men meet, consult and. place before the public better ones.

I have named the three gentlemen at the head of this chapter in the order of my estimate of their ability.

Bennett and Howard are the ripest scholars on the Pacific Coast. As ardent students to-day as they have been all their lives, they have acquired a fullness of reading—digesting what they have read —surpassed by few in America. As a jurisconsult, Bennett has never had his superior, if equal, in the State. Moreover, he is in full sympathy with the great reform movement now commencing. The plundercrats would rather have any man in the State on that Bench than him. The vulgar and vindictive assailment of these unpurchasable citizens, by the entire pack of plundercratic organs, should counsel their selection by the Workingmen's Convention.

That Howard and Terry committed a political blunder in associating themselves so intimately with the *Chronicle* since the 7th of May, and thereby antagonized a portion of the Workingmen's party to them, is true. But this should be overlooked, since the good of the Commonwealth demands that such men shall be placed upon that Supreme tribunal. Who are their superiors for the station ?

When the Plebeians of Rome had secured their proper share in the government, they made their first selection of Tribunes, and, generally, the same subsequently from the Patrician ranks—choosing such from that few who had always sympathized with them in their oppressions, and who had proved themselves more competent for such station than any in the Plebeian ranks.

Let the Workingmen imitate their example by nominating such Patricians as Bennett, Howard and Terry—Patricians by virtue of their intrinsic merit—their high moral and intellectual qualities.

R.

KEARNEY AND KEARNEYISM.

The efforts of the plundercrats to prove Denis Kearney both fool and knave, and thereby break up the Workingmen's Party, is manifestation of profound ignorance on their part, as to the character of the movement. If Kearney, as they allege, has nearly run his race, it but proves he has fulfilled the part allotted to him in the providential ordering of affairs. Let him pass away; yet this great upheaving popular tide of discontent, and the loud demand of change for the better, will surge onward with increasing momentum. Other leaders will be selected who can better personify the hopes and aspirations, and more surely lead to victory this multitudinous throng.

The character of the ticket presently to be made up, will demonstrate whether Kearney and his advisers are longer fit to head such movement. Kearney may be extinguished soon, but, so-called, Kearneyism, as sneeringly denominated, which is a vital force in society, will go on conquering and to conquer by whatsoever name it may be known.

S.

COUNSELING, HOROSCOPING AND HOPING.

I end this lenghty olio *brochure* by republishing the addendum to a pamphlet-published

"*Letter to JNO. A. EAGAN, Secretary of the Amador Miner's League;*" dated "*San Francisco, August 12th, 1871,*" and preface the same with a few more words:

The letter was drawn forth as a denunciatory protest against the pusillanimous subserviency of Governor Haight, at the behests of certain capitalists of this city, in suddenly ordering Col. Barnes and his regiment to proceed to Amador County, to quell certain reported disturbances of miners on a wage strike. The extract, including my peculiar syle of signature, and the short foot-note, are copied verbatim.

All hail ! the advent of this foreshadowed approximating storm era. Better that holicausts of human victims be sacrificed than that the present grossly demoralized condition of affairs in our land shall continue. Let the race of pigmies, who have been so long misruling, be cast aside, and giant MEN be chosen to take their places. Hail!

all hail! the glorious revolution which is destined to accomplish this great and good result, bloody though it may be. It is an event I have long been hoping for, praying for and predicting. For many years, the Devil or spirit of evil, has prompted the people to choose their leaders; hencesoon, God, or the spirit of good, will inspire them to such action.

(Extract.)

ADDENDUM.

The foregoing document is only addressed to the Amador Miners' League, because of the recent prominency gained by its semi-revolting against associated and co-operating Capital. This counter organizing and co-operating of Numbers and Necessity, against associated Capital and Cunning, is going on all over Christendom, and destined soon to be the all-absorbing issue of the age. That any peaceful settlement of the conflict can be brought about, is not for a moment entertained by me or any one possessing the smallest knowledge of history and the nature of man.

That the struggle for the mastery, will bo a fierce and bloody one, must be apparent to all who reflect upon the unscrupulous selfishness and power of Capital, and the command it has over modern politicians and office-holders—especially in a Republic; and tho ability and willingness to employ a hireling soldiery to execute the unjust and venal laws its bribes secure the passage of and decidement in their favor.

Therefore, let all who would array themselves against this poisoning and impoverishing robber rule of Wealth, be up and doing. Organize yourselves into Associations, Councils, Leagues and Clubs, military and otherwise; let there be an universal concertment between these, throughout all countries. Here in our, at present, falsely boasted land of liberty, has this soulless and decivilizing rule of the vulgar and unprincipled wealthy, had, for near the third of a century (increasing yearly its power), a more absolute sway than in any country upon the globe. Only our sparse population, wide area of virgin soil† and unparalleled resources, have prevented, long since, a subvertment of such direful dominancy.

Who will be the victors in the approaching contest, can well be prophecied by him who, having faith in the ultimate triumph of truth, comprehends the might of moral forces over the mere material; and notices that the noblest intellects and characters—the men of PRINCIPLE—are everywhere articulating fearlessly in defense of the misgoverned and defrauded masses.

CHARLES EDWARD PICKETT,
For thirty years an unawed, uncompromising and continuous assailant of the exploiting Moneycracy, and their co-operating congeners, the trafficing Politicians.

---

†The only virgin soil of this vast estate, now left for pioneer pre-emptors, consists of sterile plains and mountain steeps ; the lordly favored monopolists having appropriated the remainder.